GILGAMESH

Also by Simon Armitage

POETRY

Zoom!
Xanadu
Kid
Book of Matches
The Dead Sea Poems
Moon Country (with Glyn Maxwell)
Cloudcuckooland
Killing Time
Selected Poems
Travelling Songs
The Universal Home Doctor
Tyrannosaurus Rex Versus the Corduroy Kid
Out of the Blue
Seeing Stars
Paper Aeroplane: Selected Poems
Still
The Unaccompanied
Sandettie Light Vessel Automatic
Magnetic Field: The Marsden Poems
Tribute: Three Commemorative Poems
LX
The Cryosphere
Hansel & Gretel
Blossomise
Dwell
New Cemetery

TRANSLATIONS

Sir Gawain and the Green Knight
The Death of King Arthur
Pearl
The Owl and the Nightingale

LYRICS

Never Good with Horses: Assembled Lyrics

PLAYS

Eclipse
Mister Heracles (after Euripides)
Jerusalem
Homer's Odyssey
The Last Days of Troy
The Odyssey: Missing Presumed Dead

FICTION

Little Green Man
The White Stuff

NONFICTION

All Points North
Gig: The Life and Times of a Rock Star Fantasist
Walking Home
Walking Away
A Vertical Art: The Oxford Lectures

GILGAMESH

A NEW VERSE TRANSLATION

Simon Armitage

Liveright Publishing Corporation

A Division of W. W. Norton & Company
Independent Publishers Since 1923

Copyright © 2026 by Simon Armitage

All rights reserved
Printed in the United States of America
First Edition

For information about permission to reproduce selections from this book,
write to Permissions, Liveright Publishing Corporation, a division of
W. W. Norton & Company, Inc., 500 Fifth Avenue, New York, NY 10110

For information about special discounts for bulk purchases, please contact
W. W. Norton Special Sales at specialsales@wwnorton.com or 800-233-4830

Manufacturing by Versa Press
Book design by Anna Oler

ISBN 978-1-63149-668-4

Liveright Publishing Corporation, 500 Fifth Avenue, New York, NY 10110
www.wwnorton.com

W. W. Norton & Company Ltd., 15 Carlisle Street, London W1D 3BS

Authorized EU representative: EAS, Mustamäe tee 50, 10621 Tallinn, Estonia

1 2 3 4 5 6 7 8 9 0

CONTENTS

Introduction ix
A Note on the Translation xxxvii

TABLET I
Gilgamesh the King, Enkidu the Man
1

TABLET II
Enemies Become Comrades
17

TABLET III
May the Gods Protect
29

TABLET IV
A Journey to War
39

TABLET V
Death and Destruction
51

TABLET VI
A Fatal Rejection
65

TABLET VII
A Death Foretold
75

TABLET VIII
A Grief Laid Bare
87

TABLET IX
The Lost Soul
97

TABLET X
To the Edge of the World
105

TABLET XI
The Hardest Lesson to Learn
121

Glossary   139
Notes   147
Bibliography   157

INTRODUCTION

One of the oldest poems in the world, *Gilgamesh* came into being around four thousand years ago. That it still exists is remarkable. That it also happens to be wonderful, dealing with eternal mysteries and resounding with contemporary relevance, is almost too good to be true. At its core, it is a story of friendship, of grief, of seeking, and of failing to escape the fact of death. For all its fantastical elements—stone oarsmen, a celestial bull, a man made from clay, the gods in their heaven—it speaks with unnerving clarity about what it means to be human. *Gilgamesh* is a poem of dazzling contrasts: set in a real landscape and imagined cosmos, filled with high fantasy and everyday practicalities, touching on heroic violence and intimate sorrow. Its enduring power comes not only from its age but from its startling emotional and psychological complexity.

INTRODUCTION

COMPOSED, WRITTEN, LOST, AND FOUND

So where did this astonishing work come from, and how has it survived? In an early verse of the poem we learn that Gilgamesh is a demigod, two-thirds immortal and one-third human. But before his name became the stuff of myth and legend, he was very probably a historical figure, one named in the List of Sumerian Kings (a text, preserved on clay tablets, documenting the mythical and historical leaders of ancient Mesopotamian city-states) as the ruler of Uruk sometime between 2800 to 2500 BCE. Over many years oral traditions and songs about his exploits would have developed before being committed to any form of writing. Around 2000 BCE the first texts relating to Gilgamesh began to appear in the Sumerian language, in Southern Babylonia. Babylon is sometimes identified as one of the "cradles of civilization," an area of southern Mesopotamia between the Tigris and Euphrates Rivers, a part of the world now known as Iraq. The region boasted numerous independent city-states such as Nippur, Shuruppak, and Larsa, each settlement arranged around the temple of a patron deity. In its day and at its height, Uruk, where the poem begins and ends, was a major center of population and quite possibly the largest "urban" area on the planet, with potentially as many as a hundred

INTRODUCTION

thousand people living within its walls and wider environs. The city is an enigmatic presence in the poem, given the way it is repeatedly referenced and how it frames or bookends the narrative, a reminder that such communities gave meaningful identity and purpose to their residents. As sustainable agriculture flourished along the riverbanks and floodplains, writing also developed, initially as an administrative tool for documentation and record keeping. Sumerian is a seemingly unique language with no apparent relationship to any other, and was expressed as writing through cuneiform (literally "wedge-shaped") script, sometimes carved in stone, sometimes inscribed in wax, but more frequently imprinted in clay with a diagonally sliced reed. The diamond- or triangular-shaped tip would be pressed into wet clay tablets to create logograms (signs or characters representing words) and syllabograms (written or drawn symbols representing syllables), and the tablets would then be left in the sun to dry or kiln-baked for a harder and more permanent finish. The tablets are often described by those who have contact with them as being like small pillows in shape, about the size of an average book, with writing on both sides. It is from this period that the first Gilgamesh poems appear, written as stand-alone episodes of the king's trials and labors that would eventually be assimilated into a longer epic and used to fill gaps in later versions. Known collectively as *The Sumerian Poems of Gilgamesh*, there are five in total: "Gilgamesh and Akka," "Gilgamesh and Huwawa," "Gilgamesh and the Bull of Heaven," "Gilgamesh and the Netherworld," and "The Death of Gilgamesh." During this period, students were required to recreate poems as part of their study of literacy, history, and what we would eventually classify as literature, and the school-system method of copying poems from one tablet to another has contributed enormously to what we have retained of *Gilgamesh* in physical form. In later eras, poems would be reproduced by master scribes and scholars, some, perhaps, seeking to further their reputations or improve their standing within a religious, royal, or political system, especially if the poem in question appeared to connect a powerful contemporary ruler with the ancient hero of a story.

Over time the Sumerian language was superseded by Akkadian, and the earliest surviving version of the combined epic appears in Akkadian cuneiform dating from the eighteenth century BCE. This rendition is known as the Old Babylonian version, or is referred to by its opening line (or "incipit") "Surpassing all other kings." Much of this poem is still unrecovered, and even within the fragments of tablets that have come to light there are substantial gaps (or "lacunae"). Always subject to reclassification and retitling, and in various states of preservation, they include the Pennsylvania tablet, the Yale tablet, the Philadelphia fragment, the Nippur

INTRODUCTION

school tablet, the Tell Harmal tablets, the Ishchali tablet, the Sippar tablet, the Sealand tablet, and other miscellaneous pieces. Versions of this poem were being created over several hundred years and copied out across many parts of the ancient Near East including Anatolia, Syria, the Levant, and Babylonia. The names they have acquired—based on their "findspots" or locations they refer to, or identifying the places where they are now housed and studied—tell their own story of dissemination and distribution, and each one has some overlapping relevance to later editions of the poem.

A man by the name of Sin-leqi-unninni is credited with creating a revised edition of the Old Babylonian poem sometime between the thirteenth and eleventh century BCE. An exorcist, apparently, trained in a number of religious and magical practices, he might also be called a scribe, a scholar, a copyist, an editor, an archivist, a ghost writer, an author, and a poet. Sin-leqi-unninni reproduced, restored, and enhanced older strands of the poem, at times transferring verses word for word and line for line, at other times paraphrasing, expanding, or embellishing sections, and occasionally introducing entirely new material. One such addition, sometimes termed the Prologue, comes (unsurprisingly) at the very beginning of the poem, where a further twenty-eight lines now precede the "Surpassing all other kings" incipit, giving the poem a new incipit of "He who saw the deep."

INTRODUCTION

This eleven- or twelve-tablet version, also referred to as the Standard Version, or Standard Babylonian Version, or the canonical version, or the classical version, or the established version, or *The Epic of Gilgamesh*, is the arrangement we now think of as the actual poem. This is the work that is meant when referred to by its shorthand title, *Gilgamesh*. Nearly all translations, including this one, use the Standard Version as the line-for-line template, and nearly all retellings of the Gilgamesh story, be they in poetry, prose, film, opera, comic book, or other art forms, follow its story and structure. It is important to remember, however, that despite being recognized as a kind of authorized or approved recension of the text, many pieces of the Standard Version tablets are still unrecovered, and many of the found fragments remain indecipherable. As a consequence, more than a fifth of the poem is still missing, and only about two-thirds of the poem can be confidently restored.

In the lifespan of *Gilgamesh*, what followed the Sin-leqi-unninni era could be described as a two-and-a-half-thousand-year unintentional hibernation. In 1850, on hearing rumors of buried antiquities, Austen Henry Layard and his assistant Hormuzd Rassam began excavating earth mounds near the modern-day city of Mosul in Iraq. What they were tunneling into turned out to be the palace or citadel complex of Nineveh (modern-day Kuyunjik), including the royal librar-

INTRODUCTION

ies of Ashurbanipal, the last great king of Assyria. Along with thousands of other inscribed documents, those libraries had once contained perhaps four copies of the *Gilgamesh* poem, all shattered and scattered following the violent sacking of Nineveh circa 612 BCE. Layard and Rassam had an immediate sense of the significance of their finds, even if they were unable to translate the cuneiform scripts themselves, and more than twenty-five thousand pieces were shipped to the British Museum in London. The *Gilgamesh* fragments were among them. They sat in a box in a storeroom for another two decades. In 1872, the young curator George Smith was categorizing and documenting some of the pieces when he came across what has become the best-known portion of a *Gilgamesh* tablet, a description of the Great Flood. The opening chapter of his book, *The Chaldean Account of Genesis*,* recalls the moment "after long and heavy work" when he recognized the text for what it was. "Commencing a steady search among these fragments, I soon found half of a curious tablet which had evidently contained originally six columns of text. . . . On looking down the third column, my eye caught the statement that the ship rested on the mountains of Nizir, followed by the account of the sending forth of the dove, and its finding no resting place and returning. I saw at

---

* George Smith, *The Chaldean Account of Genesis* (London: Sampson, Low, Marston, Searle and Rivington, 1876).

INTRODUCTION

once that I had here discovered a portion at least of the Chaldean account of the Deluge."

The fact that a (very convincing) mounted resin model of the tablet can be purchased in the British Museum shop is testament not just to its renown within the Gilgamesh community but also to its status as one of the crown jewels of the museum's artifacts. The accompanying commentary reads, "A replica of one of our most famous cuneiform tablets from Mesopotamia, inscribed with the Babylonian account of the Flood as part of *The Epic of Gilgamesh*. The object caused a sensation when it was first deciphered in the nineteenth century because of its similarity to the Flood story in the Book of Genesis." In other words, here was source material for one of the best-known stories of the Old Testament, and evidence, perhaps, of the historical veracity of the event. In the Victorian era, in a Christian context, this was nothing short of mind-blowing, and the discovery made the national press. Even to a man of science like Smith, encountering such material and realizing the magnitude of its implications seems to have stimulated emotions beyond the usual scholarly reactions. His response, as later described by E. A. Wallace Budge,* is quoted in almost every commentary dealing with the deciphering of the poem, but bears repeating. Smith was decoding lines on the cleaned

---

* E. A. Wallis Budge, *The Rise and Progress of Assyriology* (London: Martin Hopkinson & Co, 1925).

and prepared tablet, "and when he saw that they contained the portion of the legend he had hoped to find there, he said, 'I am the first person to read that after two thousand years of oblivion.' Setting the tablet on the table, he jumped up and rushed about the room in a great state of excitement, and, to the astonishment of those present, began to undress himself!"

A POEM OF THEN AND NOW

In the century and a half that has followed, there have been countless translations and interpretations of *Gilgamesh*, published in many languages, and the sense of exhilaration and astonishment that Smith experienced has found its echo in readers and audiences ever since. Rainer Maria Rilke fell under its spell, declaring it to be one of language's greatest ever achievements, and his passion for this "stupendous" poem finds its way onto the covers and blurbs of many editions as a kind of five-star endorsement by a high-value poetic influencer. Clearly its antiquity is part of its hypnotic fascination, the sense that the poem carries intimations of the elemental and the primordial, a window on a world where writing, let alone literature, was still in an embryonic phase, a kind of message in a bottle, time capsule, or treasure chest dating back to the origins of civilization.

INTRODUCTION

Gilgamesh explores themes of power, loyalty, love, and loss, and does so within the narrative of a long journey and extraordinary adventures. What begins as a heroic quest for earthly glory transforms into an ultimately futile search for immortality. Nothing less than the irresolvable riddle of human existence is at stake, but alongside profound philosophical enquiries the poem is memorable for its sharp details and intense observations: exquisite jewelry, maggoty corpses, superbly crafted weapons, a magical forest alive with the calls of beasts and birds. On one level *Gilgamesh* is set in the real world, against a verifiable geography, within a traceable past, dealing with situations, emotions, actions, and reactions that are as familiar to us today as they were in their age. On another level, the poem takes us into a dimension of fantasy where warriors are capable of superhuman feats; where monsters lurk; where life can be created from lumps of clay; and where gods sit in judgment over the human race, incapable of restraint and neutrality, always meddling in the affairs of mortals, often with catastrophic results. As well as instructing us on aspects of ancient mythology and shedding some light on Mesopotamian mindsets, such departures from reality remind us that human experience isn't restricted to the bricks and mortar of quotidian life. The imagination must also be served and honored, and the pantheon of deities we encounter in the poem, along with a tusked ogre,

INTRODUCTION

oarsmen made of stone, and scorpion-headed sentries, are recreations of our dreams, desires, and fears.

At its core, the poem tells of the friendship between two people: Gilgamesh, the ruler of Uruk-the-Sheepfold and son of the goddess Ninsun, and Enkidu, a wild man of the countryside. But it is also a poem of many other characters: Ishtar, a goddess of love and war; Uta-napishti, survivor of the Great Flood; Humbaba, the terrifying guardian of the Cedar Forest; and dozens more. As well as by name and title, and with broadbrush strokes, they could also be described in terms of their roles in the story: the megalomaniac hero, the proud and worried mother, the loyal sidekick, the jilted lover, the sagacious elder, and so on. They are archetypes, we might think (literally, given the age of the poem), and they play their parts admirably. Yet at crucial moments in the story, they act capriciously, making unforeseen choices, with unexpected consequences.

No matter how much of a caricature the tyrannical Gilgamesh might first appear, a reader new to the poem would be unlikely to anticipate his deep feelings toward Enkidu—a being created to oppose him—or predict his behavior in the Cedar Forest, or his response to Ishtar's advances, or his reaction to seeing a dead body in a state of decay. The genius of the poem is that it conveys a sense of the protagonist's own uncertainty, so that every episode or scene feels as much of a revelation to us as it does to Gilgamesh. As well as in its topicality, then, it is through subtle and sophisticated storytelling that the poem exudes an air of modernity, as if we were reading a piece of writing composed by a single author familiar with contemporary literary practices. In other words, its style, as much as its subject matter, makes this ancient poem an essential text for our time.

THE TABLETS—A TALE IN ELEVEN EPISODES

Humans are often described as a storytelling species, and as much as anything *Gilgamesh* is a story. Its events, and the effect of those events, are what give the poem its forward propulsion; the eleven tablets can be thought of as poetic chapters, each one informed by what has gone before and determining what follows. The setting, at the opening of Tablet I, is Uruk-the-Sheepfold, a "city," which is also a place of worship, a stronghold, and a secure enclosure, surrounded by wilderness and wasteland. Many miles to the west lies the magical Cedar Forest. In the other direction a traveler will eventually encounter the Mountains of Mashu, the Garden of the Gods, and the Waters of Death, before arriving at the end of the world. Deities reside above and below, inhabiting both the sky and the underworld.

INTRODUCTION

This dualism between the known and the unknown is one of the central motifs of the poem, on the one hand reinforcing its sense of certainty and realism, on the other creating doubt and ambiguity. Gilgamesh, both mortal and divine, seems to embody that polarity, and from the outset he is a divided individual, in need of healing and completion. If dualism is constantly at work in the poem, so is parallelism, and in Enkidu both concepts are in operation simultaneously. Enkidu is made as a match for Gilgamesh, equal to him in strength and power, and with a corresponding storm in his heart. There are moments of both physical and emotional entanglement when the two men seem as one, or when they present as siblings, even twins. But Enkidu has no human forbears and no family. He is an "Adam," created without parentage. That his transformation to civilized human is achieved by sexual intercourse is deeply ironic, given that he was neither conceived nor born. So, for all the similarities and overlapping between them, the two characters are also opposites: one a near-Neanderthal roaming the hills with wild animals, the other a king above kings enjoying royal privileges (though to some extent their roles are reversed over the course of the poem, Enkidu experiencing the underworld in ways usually reserved for those of higher status, untamed and unkempt Gilgamesh wandering the wilderness in grief). Very different lives destined for the same human fate; in the intertwining of

INTRODUCTION

their separate strands there is something of the double helix about Gilgamesh and Enkidu.

At the beginning of Tablet II, the two men are about to square up to each other. Descriptions of their muscle power and prowess in combat might lead us to believe that this could be a fight to the death, or that the irresistible force and the immovable object might cancel each other out. By the end of the tablet the two men are not just reconciled but have become firm friends, and by the end of Tablet III they are as brothers, Ninsun having announced her intention to make Enkidu a family member. At some point in this sequence of events, and without prompting, Gilgamesh announces that the two new comrades will go to the Cedar Forest to kill Humbaba. No convincing reason is given. Gilgamesh offers some brief justification in terms of making an eternal name for himself, and later on talks about ridding the world of evil, though there is no evidence in what we have of the poem that Humbaba is anything other than the guardian of the sacred trees. He might be an ugly-looking brute, but as a protector of the natural world he seems an undeserving target, especially to environmentally conscious contemporary readers. More interesting is the role of the gods in this matter, hardly innocent in their involvement. Ninsun herself indicts Shamash, the god of the sun, for burdening her son with a restless heart, and at one point Gilgamesh talks

INTRODUCTION

about Humbaba as the enemy of Shamash, whom Gilgamesh appears keen to please.

It is becoming apparent by now that for all their power, the gods have little control over the outcomes of their interventions. Enkidu was brought to life to quell Gilgamesh's unruly impulses. Instead the gods created a two-headed problem, doubly dangerous and beyond restraint, despite Enkidu's reservations about the proposed mission. Rather than temper Gilgamesh's violent instincts the divine beings have inflamed them, exacerbating his fearlessness. Gilgamesh might be his own worst enemy, but the deities of the pantheon have seriously mishandled their attempts to curb his behavior or teach him a lesson, and the story is about to tip into carnage and chaos. Latter-day secular audiences might be skeptical about moral dilemmas or cautionary tales in which higher powers play a primary role. But even if the gods are nothing more than creations of the human imagination, they still have meaning and significance in the story, as characterful representations of unpredictable forces, like the weather, disease, or ill fortune, and as manifestations of the subconscious mind.

With their friendship forged both in the heart and over the blacksmith's anvil, and with the reluctant consent of the people of Uruk and a mother's anxious goodbyes, the two compatriots head for the Cedar Forest. If the Gilgamesh

INTRODUCTION

story foreshadows later epic poems from other eras and cultures, as some have noticed, their journey certainly becomes something of an odyssey at this point, and with the slaughter of Humbaba in Tablet V Odysseus's blinding of Polyphemus comes to mind, a similarly incendiary event. The Cyclops is the gruesome son of the god Poseidon, who pursues a vendetta against Odysseus to the end of his travels; Humbaba is the gruesome steward of the trees, appointed by the god Enlil, who will insist on punitive justice. Of the expedition itself, the trance-like repetitive nature of the poetry through this section has a peculiar effect. In some ways it enacts the mundane regularity of a long slog across featureless terrain, while in other ways it speaks of the terrific distances being covered without any let up in speed or sapping of stamina. The days have a dreamlike quality, but the dreams are uneventful compared with those Gilgamesh suffers each night, which are closer to nightmares. Why Enkidu should be able to interpret the visions when Gilgamesh, someone who "possessed all knowledge," cannot is explained in terms of Enkidu's upbringing. A connection is being made between the wilderness and the unknown. Enkidu was born in the outlands but is now a best friend of the King of Uruk, perhaps even a member of its metropolitan elite and courtly inner circle, and as someone with a foot in both camps is assumed to be some kind of intermediary.

INTRODUCTION

Gilgamesh is in uncharted territory here, both figuratively and literally, as the two men begin to penetrate the dense vegetation. As a general rule, in most stories when characters enter the forest, something changes, and when the natural morphs into the supernatural it rarely bodes well. This is true from Hansel and Gretel to *Heart of Darkness*, from *Sir Gawain and the Green Knight* to *Game of Thrones*, and in each case it always feels a little harsh on the oaks and limes etc., large biomass profusions that are only getting on with their job of growing toward the light and turning carbon dioxide into oxygen.

Despite the gaps and omissions in Tablet V, the poem describes how Gilgamesh and Enkidu both goad and encourage each other as they tread warily forward through the tangled thickets and beneath the canopy of cedars. The stillness, the sanctity, the wonder, and the natural beauty of the woods are a studied contrast to the massacre that follows. Both men show fear, both men show fortitude. For such an apparent monster Humbaba proves himself capable of logical debate and reasoned pleading, but once Shamash has directed the winds of the world into his face the die is cast, and Enkidu in particular speaks with a bloodthirsty desire. In the aftermath of the killing and in their ambition to appease Enlil by building a great door for his temple in Nippur, the two murderers bring destruction to the forest itself. By the end of the episode they have triumphed in their stated ambition, but the poem is wiser than the characters within it, and an atmosphere of disgrace and desecration hangs over the broken trees. To the modern audience, parallels with contemporary events are easily drawn, be they the decimation of the world's ancient rainforests, the mistreatment of wild animals, military raids in distant countries, jungle warfare, political assassinations, disastrous foreign policy decisions, the violent clashes between devotees of different gods, or the furious confrontations between people of opposing cultural beliefs.

As well as being largely intact, Tablet VI is probably the most clearly defined, set-piece section of the poem. The first half is mostly speech or dialogue between Gilgamesh and Ishtar, patron deity of Uruk, and the daughter of Anu, the father of the gods. It reads almost as a theater script and is notable for its humor, Gilgamesh reveling in a tirade of insults and slurs as he reels off the list of Ishtar's romantic casualties. Gilgamesh's tour-de-force riposte to Ishtar's request for his hand in marriage isn't entirely indefensible. The goddess of love is also the goddess of war, and on the domestic front she appears to have combined the two roles on numerous occasions; most of her former partners have been demeaned, assaulted, injured, or killed. The scene then escalates into an action sequence worthy of a graphic novel or fantasy comic as the Bull of Heaven is released, only to be slain by Gilgamesh and Enkidu in a strategic pincer movement. And the all-conquering king of Uruk was always going to defend himself against an attack from a raging bull, celestial or otherwise. When Enkidu throws the bull's intestines at Ishtar and threatens her with the same fate, sacrilege can be added to the crimes of pomposity and arrogance. The two men are drunk on power, drunk on success, and seemingly intoxicated by their newfound friendship. Why does Gilgamesh need a wife or even a lover when his "bromance" with Enkidu seems so fulfilling?

The actual nature of the relationship between Gilgamesh and Enkidu is a much-debated subject, and new perspectives have found their voice as society has changed since the poem was first translated against a background of nineteenth-century Western morality. That is not to say the poem speaks directly and uncontestably of a physical attraction between the two men, much as it remains a possibility. For some, Gilgamesh loving Enkidu "like a wife" is an unequivocal declaration of a same-sex physical union, especially when words that follow are translated as "caressing and embracing him."*
Alternatively, if a sexual bond does exist between Enkidu and Gilgamesh, the poem is somewhat coy or restrained in its

---

* A. R. George, "Standard Babylonian I," *Poem of Gilgameš*, with contributions by E. Jiménez and G. Rozzi, translated by Anmar A. Fadhil, Andrew R. George, and Wasim Khatabe, electronic Babylonian Library, 2022, https://doi.org/10.5282/ebl/l/1/4.

descriptions of their closeness, in contrast with the explicit account of Enkidu's seduction by Shamhat. To love someone like a wife could simply mean to love them as dearly and as deeply, through holding and hugging, rather than implying a romantic coupling. It should also be noted that the ambiguous or contentious lines in the poem are spoken by not Gilgamesh but Shamhat, recounting the words of Gilgamesh's mother, and are offered as analogy, during the interpretation of a dream. In the end, we might decide that what the poem brings into play is a consideration of the word "love," its definitions, its boundaries, and its types, a subject still under discussion so many thousands of years later. Ultimately the poem is enigmatic or vague in its meaning but prescient in its enduring themes, and whatever the connection between the two men, Ishtar has recognized the deep bond between them. Having failed to inflict physical pain on Gilgamesh via the horns and hoofs of the Bull of Heaven, she now wishes a greater punishment on her tormentor, that of grief, an emotion he does not seem to have experienced before. It is a calculated and sophisticated retaliation; soon afterward Enkidu falls ill.

A study of dreams in *Gilgamesh* would prove an absorbing undertaking. In the poem they are usually prophesies and rarely wrong, proving far more reliable than the hopes of humans and the ambitions of the divine beings. So when

INTRODUCTION

Enkidu has visions of the gods discussing his fate, and further visions of the Netherworld, we can be confident that his days among the living are numbered. Shamash knows it, and even Gilgamesh—not an interpreter of dreams, as we have learned—realizes the significance of such hallucinations. The poem has entered a new phase here, moving from action and incident to introspection and reflection. If we have been witnesses to the workings of the two men's minds and the power of their bodies, we are now about to look deep into their hearts. Tablet VII is Enkidu's great deathbed scene. His railing against the trapper and against Shamhat, the two people responsible for his civilizing, brings to mind Yeats's line "Man has created death." If it is true that human beings are the only species on earth to have foreknowledge of their own demise, Enkidu was spared the burden of that terror until he was brought into the realm of consciousness. But having vented his anger, his acquiescence toward a more generous and even serene state of mind is incredibly moving, as is his final thought, which seems to be one of acceptance, even if he had hoped for a nobler or more heroic end. Thousands of years later death is no less bewildering to humankind, no matter that we have split the atom and walked on the moon. As uncomfortable as it might be, there is no more relatable subject; we will all die, and most of us will experience the death of a loved one. At the passing of his dearest friend, perhaps his only friend, Gilgamesh throws himself into ceremony and ritual, his exquisite and colorful offerings to the gods providing a dramatic contrast to the inert body he refuses to hand over for burial. His instruction to his workforce to create an extravagant effigy of Enkidu is reminiscent of those latter-day bereaved families or individuals who set up charities or appeals or campaigns, sometimes out of a sense of helplessness, sometimes to correct perceived wrongs, and sometimes for more complex psychological reasons. Doing nothing hurts more than the distraction of doing something, and in Gilgamesh's case there is a sense in which a statue fashioned from insensate materials could bring Enkidu back to life. And why not, because after all, he was created from a lump of clay.

The last three tablets, grouped together, could be thought of as the final trimester of *Gilgamesh*. Journeys and encounters will be the themes as the broken man rambles eastward toward the end of the world. But before he embarks, and across the unspoken divide between Tablet VIII and Tablet IX, there has been a notable shift in emphasis in relation to Gilgamesh's grief. Through dread of his own death a note of self-pity now sounds in the wailing, sobbing, keening sorrow that causes the king to rip off his clothes and pull out his hair. And a speech that was part encomium, part elegy, and part command to the people, animals, and landmarks of

INTRODUCTION

Uruk instructing them how to mourn the passing of Enkidu, now includes the question "Must I die too?" In pursuit of an answer, or more specifically to try and find a way of avoiding his own demise, Gilgamesh sets off immediately in search of Uta-napishti, sole survivor of the Great Flood, a human granted divine status by the gods.

While it is true that the heartache of loss still darkens Gilgamesh's spirit, the object of his quest is in relation to his own life, and this sets up an interesting circular paradox. Enkidu's passing has made Gilgamesh aware that his existence will come to a physically repugnant end one day, hence his search for immortality. But that life will be one of unbearable mourning, lamentation, and wandering the plains in a lion's pelt, an agony from which the only escape is death. And so on, and so forth. It is a dichotomy that will take Gilgamesh to the end of his journey and the end of the poem, trying to outrun the sorrow behind him, and being drawn forward by the lure of immortality. The landscape from here on in is an obstacle course: a wilderness of prowling beasts, a pitch-black tunnel through the mountain of night, and a channel of flesh-paralyzing water. Despite everything, Gilgamesh carries his unreformed self with him; his instinct on being shown the whereabouts of Ur-shanabi and the Stone Oarsmen is to attack the former and destroy the latter. As Ur-shanabi points out, Gilgamesh is a fool to himself, behaving in a manner that leaves him further from his goal. At each destination someone or something, be it a god, goddess, or talking scorpion, advises him to turn around. And even when the raw physical challenges are completed there are psychological tests to overcome, such as staying awake for a week. At times it feels like Gilgamesh is being put through his paces, taken to the limits of bodily endurance and mental toughness. His brute strength rarely fails him, but in his mind he is found wanting, falling asleep in an instant, and later, losing the hard-won object of his mission while he bathes.

In the face of such frailties the life everlasting seems more unrealizable than ever, but Gilgamesh does not accept defeat until the very end. Before that we have the poem's major flashback scene: a telling of the Flood story, necessary to verify Uta-napishti's credentials and explain his relevance to the story, the Noah-like character and his wife being the only people on the planet to whom the word *antediluvian* can be properly applied. To practiced readers familiar with the pace and structure of modern stories, it feels odd that with only a few dozen lines left Gilgamesh is nowhere near succeeding or failing in his mission; the memorable incident with the snake is yet to happen, and a satisfactory resolution to the whole epic seems unrealizable. Certainly the poem cannot be accused of laboring its conclusion, though in relation to the snake it's possible that we assign the incident more signifi-

INTRODUCTION

cance, seeing it, as we do, through the lens of the Christian Bible, than it might have had to its contemporary audience. In the Book of Genesis the serpent is responsible for nothing less than the fall of mankind, tempting Eve with the apple and causing the first humans to be evicted from Paradise—where presumably they would have lived eternally. In the poem the reverse happens; rather than offering fruit, the snake steals a plant, and robs Gilgamesh of the possibility of immortality. Snakes shed their skin, so as well as providing a dramatic plot point the incident is also presented as a zoological creation myth, explaining how serpentine creatures are able to renew themselves and apparently live forever. In the poem, the whole incident is dealt with in a handful of lines.

Stuck with the skin he was born in, Gilgamesh throws up his arms in despair, and after a foreshortened journey retracing his footsteps, he arrives back in Uruk with Ur-shanabi, the ferryman, who is now a passenger on the road to Mesopotamia rather than a pilot toward the life everlasting. The poem reverts to its prologue, bookending the story, but offers no report in respect of its meaning. Gilgamesh has returned home defeated in his impossible quest but, we suppose on his behalf, a wiser human being. Rather than a gateway to eternity, Uruk stands before him as a testament to earthly reality.

It is at this point, and from this end of history, that the circumstantial outer life of the poem once again overshadows its intended inner life. Enkidu, a being made from clay, lives on in the clay tablets the poem is written on, exhumed after hundreds and hundreds of years of lying buried in the earth. And Gilgamesh, having failed to achieve his hopes of outwitting death, has become one of the most long-lived characters in literary history, gaining vitality and fame with every retelling of his story.

A NOTE ON THE TRANSLATION

Imagine a jigsaw. But instead of a photograph of a pretty lake or snowy hillside, imagine the picture is a poem. A long poem. Then imagine many such jigsaws, manufactured over hundreds of years, all showing similar versions of the same poem but created by different makers, and cut into different patterns. Then imagine that the jigsaws, made out of clay, have been tipped from their boxes and scattered to the earth, and that the scatterings took place more than two thousand years ago, across several thousand square miles, in war-torn and battle-scarred lands, and that the poem in the picture is written in an obsolete language. The analogy isn't perfect, but it serves to give an impression of the scale and scope of the problem facing any would-be translator of *Gilgamesh*. A sizeable proportion of the poem is still missing, and what we do possess—seventy-some fragments, or "manuscripts"—is in bits.

All translation is an illusion. The only true translation of any piece of writing is a perfect facsimile of the original, letter for letter. In other words, no translation at all. When writ-

A NOTE ON THE TRANSLATION

ing is exported from one language and imported into another, unintended changes take place. No word has an exact counterpart in another language, because all words carry psychological baggage and subliminal meaning belonging to their cultures and contexts, insinuations and inferences that rarely, if ever, transfer conveniently across linguistic borders or over periods of time. Even within their own territories and despite the best efforts of dictionaries to define and circumscribe, words can be unstable and contrary units. In literary translation there is, perhaps, something of a spectrum or sliding scale, with highly educated attempts at accuracy and faithfulness at one end, and freestyle versioning at the other. But never outright perfection. When it comes to poetry this is especially true, and more so in the case of *Gilgamesh*, a poem in a permanent state of evolution.

That is not to diminish intellectual and academic renditions of the poem, far from it. In fact without such painstaking and scrupulous investigations by experts in the field—some of whom have made the poem the object of their life's work—we would have no *Gilgamesh* whatsoever. We might think of these editions as restorations, piece-by-piece philological reconstructions of the ruins of the poem, as much archaeological endeavors at times as literary ones. Readers already acquainted with the poem will probably be familiar with this form of presentation, where every gap and omission

A NOTE ON THE TRANSLATION

is honored though fastidious punctuation and where elaborate systems of annotation are installed within the text to indicate provenance. These translations can be as perplexing as they are fascinating. They convey a deep sense of respect, knowledge, and authenticity, while giving the appearance of material that is yet to be processed. At times, when faced with such forensically assembled recreations, the impression given is more like a spreadsheet than a poem, or data beamed back from a space probe many years and miles into its voyage. There is something both stunningly precise and bewilderingly abstract about such renderings, as if they are meticulously crafted translations . . . awaiting translation.

Andrew George is arguably the foremost authority on the poem and an enthusiastic advocate on its behalf, always keen to promote interest in the work and in Assyrian studies generally. Without his rigorous analysis of the tablets, his unparalleled critical commentaries, and indeed his published translations, many other translations—including this one—would not be possible. Or would be very different. But I disagree with him when he writes that "no adult reader is well served"* by modern editors who gloss over or fuse together disconnected fragments of the poem. This cannot be true for those grown-up readers who have enjoyed Stephen Mitchell's

---

* *The Epic of Gilgamesh*, trans. Andrew George (Penguin, 1999).

A NOTE ON THE TRANSLATION

streamlined "new English version,"* where no textual omissions are acknowledged and where the author has reshaped lines and passages to suit his style and purpose, going "off-grid" at times rather than following the original line for line. Or readers who came to *Gilgamesh* through N. K. Sandars's 1960 prose version† (George was one of them), some of which now seems "wrong" in light of recent research, but which still has a life force and spirit of its own. Sandars makes the apparently unpardonable error of appending "The Death of Gilgamesh" to the story, not considered part of the Standard Version, though to a general reader it makes more sense than attaching Tablet XII, in which Enkidu is once again alive. Or those readers who have loved, as I have, Jenny Lewis's impressionistic *Gilgamesh Retold*, "a response to the ancient epic,"‡ as it rolls through its shifting forms and succeeds in its objective "to engage with the epic at a subliminal level rather than treat it with too much reverence as a historical artefact."

Besides which, is the inclusion of rows and rows of dots, or other typographic symbols (or even empty pages, as some translators prefer), really a convincing representation of missing pieces of clay inscribed with cuneiform writing? Surely engaged readers are capable of imagining such gaps with

---

* *Gilgamesh, A New English Version*, trans. Stephen Mitchell (Profile Books, 2004).
† *The Epic of Gilgamesh*, trans. N. K. Sandars (Penguin, 1960).
‡ *Gilgamesh Retold*, trans. Jenny Lewis (Carcanet, 2018).

A NOTE ON THE TRANSLATION

only a minimal amount of intervention or disruption to their reading experience. Benjamin R. Foster, another esteemed academic author who has made significant contributions to the study and translation of the poem, goes further than George when he says, "I have no patience with clueless folk who think they can translate the epic without going to the trouble of mastering Babylonian."* This is a disheartening and discouraging comment. Are we really to accept that satisfactory transmissions of the Gilgamesh story rest entirely in the hands of professionals in the subject of Assyriology, or that the poem is located behind some kind of intellectual force field, or that those of us outside the inner circle must leave such profound work to the fellowship? And what of the counter argument: that the job of translating poetry cannot be fully realized by professors, only by poets?

Echoing George and Foster to some extent, Michael Schmidt comments, "Interlopers achieve mixed results among the dead languages of the world."† Am I one such interloper, trespassing on hallowed ground? My approach to *Gilgamesh* has been the same as for my medieval translations, with the hope of producing critically informed work that speaks to the

---

* Iclal Vanwesenbeeck, "Translating Gilgamesh: A Conversation with Benjamin Foster," *World Literature Today*, January 10, 2017.
† Michael Schmidt, *Gilgamesh: The Life of a Poem* (Princeton University Press, 2019).

A NOTE ON THE TRANSLATION

widest readership, attempting to balance linguistic and historical frameworks against literary expectations of the present day. The difference this time is that like almost everyone else on the planet I have no comprehension of Akkadian or other languages of the period, and for his thorough and no-nonsense translations of the cuneiform scripts I am indebted to Jacob L. Dahl, professor of Assyriology and fellow of Wolfson College, Oxford, who provided me with the literals to work from. Jacob also answered hundreds, perhaps thousands, of my questions, some of them well below his pay grade, and stuck to the task for three or four more years beyond my wildly optimistic timeframe. I am enormously grateful to Jacob, for being a medium between this world and the world of the long dead, and for help in bringing them back to life. Any errors of judgment or rogue deviations between the files he submitted to me and the publication of this book are entirely of my making.

In relation to the depleted text, I decided to try and judge every omission on its merits, or lack of them. Some small gaps are relatively inconsequential; these are indicated as line numbers within square brackets, recognizing the absence of translatable script while trying not to distract from the onward flow of the poem. The same method has been employed to denote longer omissions—sometimes thirty or forty lines at a time—where the missing text cannot sensibly be recreated

A NOTE ON THE TRANSLATION

or imagined. However, other lacunae, by virtue of surrounding context or implied meaning, seem to invite a speculative response, or can be filled in from parallel material. The impulse to mend the fractured text here and there is not an attempt to mislead readers or to give the impression of a fully formed original. It comes out of a desire, and possibly a duty, as a poet, to create something coherent and rewarding, similar to the impulses and responsibilities Sin-leqi-unninni might have felt when assembling a living, compelling epic from dispersed and diverse sources. To introduce new words to such a revered poem will be seen by some as impudence bordering on impiety. Perhaps it is, and let Enlil judge me. But bridging and spanning those gaps was also something of a thrill. A metaphorical case of getting the poem to skate across thin ice, or traverse fissures, or perform some kind of high-wire act over areas of unavailable or incomprehensible text, even if it will be judged by some as "papering over the cracks." My initial impulse was to signal the mends and darns through the deployment of italics, but switching typefaces so often (sometimes two or three times in a line) created exactly the kind of optical and cerebral disturbance I was intent on avoiding. So after assiduously applying that system across hundreds of lines and thousands of words, and rigorously cross-checking my work against critical editions of the poem, I removed all italics inside the main body of the poem

A NOTE ON THE TRANSLATION

with a couple of keystrokes—and felt better for it. It is absolutely right to recognize the poem's inherent incompleteness, but not improper, I believe, to favor readability and a sense of poetic wholeness over the worship of its accidental breakages. In his 2021 translation of *Gilgamesh*,* in an attempt to "stake out a middle way" between "poetic power" and "philological exactitude," Sophus Helle removes all the brackets and parentheses that clutter some conscientious translations, but uses a system of raised dots and empty space to imply gaps in the script. One person's middle way is another person's twisting chicane, and what counts as the middle ground will always be a nuanced matter including personal judgement and taste. And this publication is not intended as a reference or critical edition of the poem—those editions are available elsewhere, intricately annotated and with extensive commentaries, notes, glossaries, and appendices.

In keeping with many other *Gilgamesh* translations, I have filled in some larger sections with material from sources older or other than the Standard Version. To differentiate, these are presented in prose. The repetitions in the poem, of which there are many, are seen by some as an annoyance, and would be unlikely to earn their keep in a contemporary poem. But to me they were non-negotiable, such reiterations

---

* *Gilgamesh: A New Translation of the Ancient Epic*, trans. Sophus Helle (Yale University Press, 2021).

of formulaic language being a notable feature of *Gilgamesh*, placing it firmly in the narrative tradition, reminding us of its oral beginnings, creating trance-like, incantatory passages, and invoking a mystique and strangeness that is difficult to explain but essential to its identity. Occasionally, though infrequently, I have intervened and made alterations to what is being articulated. For example, in Tablet V, line 202 as well as expressing concern that they might have enraged Enlil by killing Humbaba, Gilgamesh and Enkidu are worried about Shamash for the same reason. There would be a reasonable explanation for this in the world of the epic, but in a twenty-first century transmission I could not make sense of such an apparent contradiction, given that Shamash was complicit in the killing, so I omitted his name from the passage. Elsewhere, for the sake of comprehension, I have felt the urge to try and write what the poem means, rather than what it says, reworking attested original material into a present-day register. Take as an example the repeated phrase "prepared his mouth to speak." To our ears there is something slightly awkward, affected, or even anatomical about such a construction of language, which may simply have been a commonly used expression meaning "he said," and I have found alternatives.

Other aspects of my approach relate to the classification of this edition as a "verse translation" rather than simply a "translation." *Gilgamesh* is a poem. It is written in verses.

A NOTE ON THE TRANSLATION

Most of its lines are contained units, like sentences, but also like bars in a musical composition. The definition of poetry is beyond the brief of this introduction (and quite possibly beyond any kind of summary) but in its form, layout, structure, cadences, metaphors, repetitions, phraseology, and implied meanings, *Gilgamesh* exhibits nearly all the traits and techniques by which we have come to recognize the art. My priority, therefore, was that this translation must also be a poem, and must find a way of being such a thing many thousands of years after it was first conceived. To begin with, then, it must have the appearance of verse, or of conventional verse, and crudely this means creating lines of roughly the same length. And managing the intervals between them, so the lines break after measured or completed clauses, not midsentence, in midair. Most of the lines in *Gilgamesh* conform to that notion, though from time to time I have had to extend lines by bringing in extra material or condense lines by excising one or two words. In a few instances, often where lines contain a great deal of information, sometimes in list form, I have doubled the length of the line and presented it in a "turned over" form (broken, and with the lower part indented) rather than have it sticking out like the proverbial sore thumb. However, the main reason for adopting this method is less about visual tidiness and more about the sound of the poem. Its rhythm, that is, or its beat. Because a

A NOTE ON THE TRANSLATION

work of this type lives by the pulse of orchestrated language, and I have fashioned the poem as far as possible in measures of four irregular beats per line. This is not designed to imitate the acoustic patterning of the original but rather to offer a contemporary equivalence. That said, when attempting to read transliterated lines out loud, I did detect a similar rhythm, as well as recognize how many lines fell into two balanced halves and seemed to revel in the playfulness and mellifluousness of alliteration. When the Gilgamesh poem was finally written down, long after it had existed in the heads and on the tongues of men and women, its scripted form would have attempted to emulate the tones of prayer, chant, song, or ritualized language that differed from everyday talk or transactional conversation. Even then it must have carried in both its matter and its manner an atmosphere of nostalgia, one that recalled the past and upheld tradition, and must have operated by techniques and devices that were well established. The lines in my translation—lines of verse—are shaped to invoke the same mood.

Finally, it is worth remembering that even among committed experts there is no absolute agreement regarding the content and configuration of the poem. On almost every aspect of its being opinion differs, from the decipherment, transcription, and translation of individual words, to the number of lines, to the nature and placement of missing frag-

A NOTE ON THE TRANSLATION

ments. There is not, and never can be, a conclusive translation of *Gilgamesh* because there is no definitive original. *Gilgamesh* has no single starting point and no place of ultimate arrival. It is a work in constant flux, to which all translations are a contribution and a continuation. It is the product of many minds, many hands, and is many poems. This is my version—a personal response to the evidence available. Even if all eleven (or twelve) tablets were unearthed intact, there will be other tablets from the same or earlier or later periods with minor discrepancies or major variations. The translation of old poetry should be a democratizing activity, making work available to new and wider readerships, preventing poems from turning to dust in the dark corners of museums and libraries, and not allowing them to become cryptograms, legible only to code-crackers and the cognoscenti. Nobody owns *Gilgamesh* because everybody owns *Gilgamesh*, and it is to everybody who might be interested that I dedicate this book.

—Simon Armitage

GILGAMESH

TABLET I

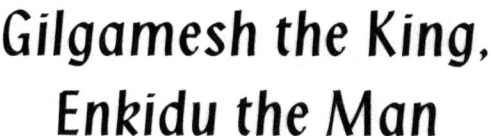

Gilgamesh the King, Enkidu the Man

Gilgamesh, demigod king of Uruk, is abusing his powers, bullying young men and imposing himself on young women. From a lump of clay the gods create Enkidu to challenge him, a wild being of the countryside who is civilized and made human through a prolonged sexual encounter with Shamhat. Gilgamesh has been dreaming about the man who will become his closest friend.

He witnessed great depths, saw the land's bedrock.
Astute in all subjects, wise in every matter,
Gilgamesh glimpsed the foundations of life.
Nothing escaped him; he possessed all knowledge,
had learned each discipline in equal measure, 5
understood completely the ways of the world.
He uncovered secrets, revealed what was hidden,
brought back word from before the Great Flood,
trudged distant paths, earned his rest.
He carved his trials and travails in a stone. 10
He constructed the fortified walls of Uruk,
and the Temple of Heaven, sacred enclosure.
Look, ramparts as straight as woolen thread,

and battlements of matchless workmanship.
Ascend the stairs, built in ancient times,
to the Temple of Heaven, the house of Ishtar—
no king will make such magnificence again.
Walk around on the upper walls of Uruk,
inspect the stronghold's solid structure.
Aren't its courses composed of kiln-baked bricks?
Were its footings not laid by the Seven Sages?
A thousand acres of dwellings and buildings,
> a thousand acres of gardens and groves,
> a thousand acres of quarries and clay pits,
> and the Temple of Heaven—five hundred acres.

Behold the extent of Uruk-the-Sheepfold!
Locate the cedar-wood storage-box,
release its locks, its bronze clasps,
raise its lid and expose its contents,
lift the lapis lazuli tablet and read
of Gilgamesh—his adventures and all he endured.
King above kings, most formidable presence.
Uruk's own hero, uncontainable wild bull,
at the front leading the march into battle,
at the rear defending his brothers-in-arms,
both secure embankment protecting his ranks
and flood surge sweeping stone walls aside.
Ox-strong offspring of Lugalbanda

and the goddess Ninsun "She-Wild-Cow."
Faultless Gilgamesh, towering and threatening,
who forged new routes through impassable mountains,
sank wells in the arid slopes of the foothills,
sailed the wide sea to where the sun rises,   40
sought eternal life at the edge of the world,
reached Uta-napishti's faraway realm.
He restored temples the Great Flood had ruined,
brought ritual and ceremony to the lost multitudes.
Who can stand as his equal or rival his right?   45
Or proclaim, as he can, "I am king above all"?
"Gilgamesh," he was called, from the day he was born,
one-third of him mortal and two-thirds divine.
His form was fashioned by Aruru, the Mother Goddess;
Ea, god of wisdom, gave him his life.   50
Magisterial in status and also in stature,
in height he measured eleven cubits,
this commanding being with the chest of a bull,
who was like no other in the thickness of his limbs.
Each of his feet was three cubits long   55
and the length of his leg was half a rod.
His stride, when he walked, reached six cubits.
The curls of his beard had the luster of gems
and flowed from his cheeks—three cubits in length.
His hair grew in sheaves, like the Goddess of Grain.   60

He had grown to become the epitome of perfection.
By all earthly measures he was deemed beautiful.
In Uruk-the-Sheepfold he swaggered about,
barging like a bull, head held high,
his weapons at the ready, so all his companions   65
were kept on their toes by the speed of his game.
Resentment grew among the young men of Uruk;
night and day he detained them from their fathers,
aggressive in his actions, swollen with arrogance.
King Gilgamesh, ruler of countless people,   70
shepherd of the flock in the sheepfold of Uruk,
but a sovereign who came between daughters and
   their mothers.
At length the long-suffering women of the city
protested their grievances and woes to the gods.
"As powerful, eminent, and intelligent as he is,   75
Gilgamesh deprives new grooms of their brides."
So said young wives and the daughters of warriors,
and the goddess Ishtar heard their complaints.
All the lords of heaven acknowledged their cries
and appealed to Anu, the god of the skies.   80
"In Uruk-the-Sheepfold you have reared a wild bull.
With his weapons poised he has no equal.
He tests the nerve of Uruk's young men
with the speed of his game, and their anger grows.

He allows no son to return to his father, 85
bristling with violence both day and night,
yet he is the shepherd in the sheepfold of Uruk,
leader of multitudes, master of their lives,
the people are his sheep and he is their shepherd,
the powerful, the eminent, the intelligent Gilgamesh. 90
No couple is spared his interference,
be they daughters of warriors or brides of young men."
Anu heard them and considered their outrage;
he summoned Aruru to hear the case.
"You, Aruru, who created humankind; 95
now shape a life to match Gilgamesh.
Let this being have an equal storm in his heart.
Let combat between them lead to peace in Uruk."
When the goddess Aruru heard these words
she conjured an image of what Anu had in mind: 100
she washed her hands, took a lump of clay
and cast it onto the grassy plain.
In that outland she created Enkidu the warrior,
birthed in silence, with Ninurta's strength.
The whole of his body was shaggy with coarse hair 105
and the locks on his head were those of a woman,
growing long and lush like the tresses of Nissaba,
a stranger to humans, of no homestead or tribe.
In a pelt, like Shakkan, god of wild animals,

he grazed on the plains with wandering herds, 110
drank with wild beasts at the water hole,
happy to live among the creatures of this world.
Then one day a hunter, setting his snares,
set eyes on this being at the water's edge.
On a second then a third day he watched him there, 115
his expression frozen with amazement and shock
as wild man and beasts went off to their den.
The hunter was silenced by fear and foreboding,
his features dimmed by the trouble in his mind,
his stomach churning with worried thoughts. 120
His face was that of a lost traveler.
He cleared his throat and said to his father:
"A stranger comes to the hollow to drink,
the mightiest in the land, of exceptional power,
as strong as the stones that fall from the sky; 125
all day he roams the foothills and plains,
grazing on grass with the antelope herds.
Near the water his footprints are a common sight.
I am too afraid to risk stealing up on him.
All the pits that I dig he fills back in. 130
Where I set up my snares he pulls them to bits.
Then he leads the herds beyond my reach.
He denies me my livelihood as a trapper in these lands."
His father gathered his thoughts and spoke:

"Go to Uruk and approach King Gilgamesh. 135
Be humble and fearful as you stand in his presence,
he is mighty, and as strong as a stone from the sky.
Set your face toward Uruk and travel that road,
he will know how to tame this intimidating stranger.
Go, son, and bring back Shamhat the courtesan; 140
her charms will civilize this man of brute strength.
When the herd gathers at the water hole
she'll disrobe and reveal her nakedness to him.
Attracted by her womanhood he'll edge toward her
and become estranged from the creatures of his
    upbringing." 145
The hunter listened to his father's wise words
and followed his advice, headed out on a journey,
set his sights on Uruk and took to the road.
Once in the city he addressed King Gilgamesh:
"An outsider drinks with beasts at the creek, 150
the mightiest in the country, powerful beyond words.
He has strength in abundance, like rocks from the heavens,
and roams the plains and the foothills all day,
grazing the grasslands with the wild herds.
His footprints are always at the hollow where he drinks. 155
I don't have the courage to sneak up behind him.
I dig pits to catch animals, but he fills them all in!
He destroys all the snares and traps that I lay!

He releases the quarry I catch from my clutches!
He will not allow me to live as a hunter." 160
Gilgamesh replied to this man of the countryside:
"Go back, and take Shamhat the courtesan,
wait by the hollow where the herd gather.
Let her take off her clothes and display her body.
When he sees her undressed he will sidle closer. 165
The beasts he lives with will soon disown him."
So the hunter left, with Shamhat at his side.
They traveled the road, covered the distance.
After three days they reached the appointed place.
Hunter and courtesan crouched down to hide, 170
waiting by the hollow for one day, then a second,
till the herd came over the plains to drink.
Many animals arrived to enjoy the water,
with Enkidu among them, whose origin was the hills,
this creature who grazed on grass with gazelles. 175
He jostled with the herd at the water hole,
quenching his thirst with the beasts of the field.
Shamhat spotted the primitive being,
a savage young brute at home in the outlands.
The hunter whispered, "Uncover your breasts 180
and open your legs; awaken his desire.
Don't be afraid. Inhale his scent.
He will notice your body and be drawn toward you.

Spread your clothes on the ground; let him lie above you
and know what it is to experience a woman. 185
Stir his passion, one human to another.
Then the creatures he calls his kin will disown him."
She emerged from the cover of reeds and undressed.
She parted her legs and he nuzzled against her.
She was not afraid; she breathed in his odor. 190
On the blanket of her clothes he lay on top of her.
She showed the wild beast the pleasures of a woman.
She made him want her, arousing his desire.
For six days and seven nights the two of them coupled
till Shamhat's excitements had drained him of his urges, 195
at which point he looked toward the herd.
The gazelles saw Enkidu but skittered away,
the creatures turned tail and headed for the plains,
the pureness of his body being tainted now.
The herd scattered but his legs would not follow, 200
he was sapped and enfeebled, the spring gone from his feet,
yet he knew more, understood more—his mind had grown.
He returned and sat down at Shamhat's feet,
gazing at her face, staring into her eyes,
listening closely to the words she spoke. 205
Shamhat the courtesan said to Enkidu:
"You are beautiful, Enkidu, godlike in appearance,
so why do you roam the plains with wild beasts?

I will take you to the heart of Uruk-the-Sheepfold,
to the holy dwelling of Anu and Ishtar, 210
to where Gilgamesh sits, that perfection of strength.
Like a wild bull he struts among the young men."
She talked of Gilgamesh, and Enkidu listened,
and his heart told him what he needed was a friend.
Enkidu spoke to Shamhat the courtesan: 215
"Lead the way, Shamhat, to Uruk-the-Sheepfold,
to the holy dwelling of Anu and Ishtar,
to the palace of Gilgamesh, that epitome of strength,
who intimidates and bullies the sons of the city.
I will stare him down, be a match for his power; 220
in the center of Uruk I'll proclaim, 'I am mightiest,'
and the future shall be changed because of my challenge.
Who is born beyond walls will never be outmuscled."
"No," replied Shamhat, "Let him see your face;
I know that a bond between you exists. 225
Follow me, Enkidu, to Uruk-the-Sheepfold,
where the men wear vibrant sashes and belts,
where festivals and feasts take place every day
and the beating of drums is a constant sound.
Where beautiful women offer their company, 230
sensuous and seductive, always promising pleasure—
even the elderly are called from their sleep!
Enkidu, who knows so little of life,

I'll present you to spirited Gilgamesh,
you will see his features, set eyes on his face. 235
His looks are striking, with a figure to be proud of,
the very embodiment of manliness and vigor.
His prodigious strength is greater than yours
and he takes no rest, neither day or night.
Enkidu, restrain your violent intent, 240
Gilgamesh is the favorite of Shamash the Sun God.
Anu, Enlil, and Ea made him wise.
Before you arrived, emerging from the hills,
you appeared in the dreams of Gilgamesh in Uruk.
He woke filled with wonder, saying to his mother: 245
'Mother, in the night I experienced this dream:
the stars of heaven were there above me,
then one fell to earth, like a meteorite.
It was far too heavy to lift and carry.
I tried to move it but it stayed put. 250
The land of Uruk was standing upon it,
settled on top of it, assembled and arranged.
Fighters were gathered, massing in the foreground.
Many young men were crowding over it,
as if they were kissing the feet of a child. 255
At that moment I loved it, hugged it like a wife.
Then I picked it up and dropped it at your feet,
and there and then you made it my equal.'

Gilgamesh's mother was wise and all-knowing.
Ninsun "She-Wild-Cow" replied to her son: 260
'The stars of heaven appeared before you.
One fell at your feet like a meteorite.
You picked it up but its weight was too great.
You tried to dislodge it but it stayed in place.
Then you raised it from the ground and dropped it where
    I stand.   265
And I, your mother, made it your equal.
And then you loved it, held it like a wife.
A comrade will come, to redeem his friend,
a man from the country, with the strength of nature,
whose might is as great as a meteorite.   270
And then you will love him, you will hold him like a wife.
By his power he will save you many times over.
Your vision was precious and a good omen.'
Then Gilgamesh woke from a second dream
    and went before his mother, the goddess,
to recount his vision, saying to his mother: 275
'I have seen in my sleep a second dream.
In the street, here in the city of Uruk,
the people assembled where an axe was thrown down,
and the land of Uruk was set out over it,
the country itself arranged about it.   280
Standing in front of it were companies of warriors

and heaped above it was a pile of young men.
I picked up the axe and threw it at your feet,
then I loved that axe, held and touched it like a wife,
and you, my mother, declared it my equal.' 285
The mother of Gilgamesh was wise in all ways;
Ninsun "She-Wild-Cow" replied to her son:
'My son, the axe you dreamed of is a man.
Like a wife you will come to love him and embrace him.
I will make him your counterpart, an equal of yours; 290
you will find in that man a comrade and rescuer.
Born in the wild he has nature's strength,
as resolute and hard as a rock from the sky.'
Gilgamesh spoke to her, saying to his mother:
'As Enlil commands, let this be my fate. 295
A counsellor and companion will come my way;
I will have in my life a guide and a friend.'
Gilgamesh had seen such things in his sleep."
Once Shamhat had described those dreams to Enkidu
the man and the woman resumed their lovemaking. 300

TABLET II

Enemies Become Comrades

Enkidu spends time in a shepherd's camp and learns the ways of humans. In Uruk he confronts Gilgamesh. The two men fight, then out of respect pledge loyalty and kinship to each other. Enkidu weeps when Gilgamesh's mother, Ninsun, describes how he is a man without family. Gilgamesh proposes an adventure: they will journey to the Cedar Forest and slay its ferocious guardian, Humbaba. They visit the forge to have armor and weapons made, although Enkidu is reluctant, and the elders of the city caution against the trip.

Enkidu was sitting at the feet of Shamhat.

For six more days and seven more nights the two of them [2–29]*
made love, until Enkidu had forgotten the ways of his
upbringing in the wilderness. Shamhat said to Enkidu,
"When I look at you, Enkidu, it is as if I am looking at

---

* In keeping with many other *Gilgamesh* translations, I have filled in some larger sections with material from sources older or other than the Standard Version. To differentiate, these sections—starting here with this reconstruction of lines 2 through 29 of Tablet II—are presented in prose. The line numbers of the missing material are noted in the margin in brackets and in italics. Elsewhere in the poem where lines are missing but a reconstruction is either inadvisable (because it would be too speculative) or unnecessary (because the flow of the text isn't harmed by the omission), I have simply noted the line numbers and left a single blank line to stand in for the gap.

a god. Why do you roam the countryside with untamed
beasts? Come with me, I will take you to Uruk-the-
Sheepfold, to the Temple of Heaven, the dwelling place
of Ishtar and Anu. Uruk is a city where young men work
hard and have fun, you will find your place there, you
will live as a human among humans. Leave the plains to
the animals and the shepherds."

He listened to his thoughts, considered his judgement.   30
His mind agreed with the words she had spoken;
his heart was filled now with knowledge and wisdom
and he felt the truth of Shamhat's lessons.
She dressed herself in one of her garments
and gave another to Enkidu, to clothe him.   35
She took his hand and led him like a god
to the shepherd's hut, at the site of a sheepfold.
All the shepherds there gathered around him,
each of them coming to the same conclusion,
that this young man had the build of Gilgamesh,   40
tall in stature, standing proud like a battlement.
"Perhaps he's a native of the mountains?" they said.
"As strong as a stone that falls from heaven."
They set down bread in front of him.
They set down beer in front of him.   45
He stared at both but touched neither:
he had never been taught how to eat bread,

ENEMIES BECOME COMRADES

he did not know how to drink beer.
Shamhat spoke to him, saying to Enkidu:
"Eat the bread, the staff of the people.   50
Drink the beer, the destiny of the land."

Enkidu ate the bread until his stomach was full. He drank   [52–58]
seven flagons of beer, until his thoughts were giddy. His
face wore a smile and in his heart he was happy. He
shaved the fur from his body, groomed his hair, and
rubbed oil into his skin. He picked up a weapon, like a
warrior, ready to face danger.

His heart was now full of wisdom and knowing;
he would slay wolves and chase away lions   60
while the head shepherd took his rest,
Enkidu the herdsman, awake and watchful.
Then a young passerby, invited to a wedding,
was heading to Uruk-the-Sheepfold for the ceremony.

Enkidu said, "Bring that man to me, I want to know   [65–99]
where he is going and what his business is." Shamhat
called to the man and he approached them. Enkidu asked
the man where he was heading in such a hurry. He said,
"I am a guest at a wedding. Such ceremonies are the way
of the people in these parts. My role is to serve delicious
food at the feast. Then after the festivities Gilgamesh

will enter the bridal chamber, and the veil of the bride
will be drawn aside, and the king will lie down with her.
Because the king will know the bride before her husband.
Because she is his by right, and the gods have decreed
it. On hearing this the blood drained from Enkidu's face.
With Shamhat he went straight to Uruk and strode boldly
into the main square. Crowds gathered around him, saying, "This man looks very much like Gilgamesh, a shorter
and stockier version of the king. They say this man was
reared by beasts, brought up in the mountains. Let the
ceremonies and revelries begin—Uruk loves its festivals.
This man will be a match for Gilgamesh. Young men,
decide who your champion will be." The nuptial bed had
been prepared and Gilgamesh was making his way to the
bridal chamber.

Enkidu stood in the street in Uruk, 100
one man alone with the strength of many,
confronting Gilgamesh, blocking his path.
The land of Uruk spread out before the king,
he stood at the center of his own country.
Guards were pushing and shoving in front of him, 105
crowds of young men elbowing and jostling,
kissing his feet as they would a baby.
God-like Gilgamesh was making his way
to a bridal chamber, to assert his right.
Already his equal had taken his position: 110
Enkidu's foot blocked the door of the house,

ENEMIES BECOME COMRADES

he refused to step aside as Gilgamesh approached.
At the threshold of the building they seized each other,
grappling and wrestling in Uruk's main thoroughfare
as the doorframe shook and the walls quaked.   115

The two men grappled and skirmished, butting and barg-   [116–161]
ing, snorting with fury like wild bulls, throwing each
other to the floor, until their strength and anger were
spent. Gilgamesh knelt above Enkidu, and the fight
was over. Enkidu said, "You are unlike any other man,
Gilgamesh. Your mother, Ninsun 'She-Wild-Cow,' gave
birth to a hero and a warrior. The god Enlil made sovereignty your destiny." The two men embraced. Enkidu
said to Shamhat, "Let me reward you for bringing me to
Uruk-the-Sheepfold and leading me along the path to the
great Gilgamesh, who is now my true friend."*

"In this land of ours he is mighty and forceful
with the power and strength of a rock from heaven
and he stands like a battlement, tall and commanding."
The mother of Gilgamesh prepared her reply,   165
readied her thoughts before making her answer.
Then Ninsun "She-Wild-Cow" spoke to her son:

[168–177]

* Lines are missing at the end of this passage. Where the text resumes, Gilgamesh is speaking, introducing or describing Enkidu to his mother.

Enkidu stood there listening to her speech,
considering her words, then he sat down and wept.
His eyes glistened, overflowing with tears,   180
his arms hung loose, all his strength was sapped.
Then the two men seized each other and hugged;
like interlocked hands the pair of them embraced.
Gilgamesh was filled with sympathy and pity;
to Enkidu he spoke these consoling words: 185
"Why, my friend, did your eyes brim with tears,
and your arms lose their strength and your power
   ebb away?"
Enkidu replied, saying to Gilgamesh:
"A fire burned in the core of my being,
sadness overwhelmed me and my body trembled,   190
fearfulness stirs in the pit of my stomach."

[192]

To Enkidu, these words came from Gilgamesh's mouth:

"Come, let's travel to the Cedar Forest and slay gruesome Humbaba. We will go to his homeland and kill him in his lair, bring an end to his reign of terror." Enkidu said to Gilgamesh, "This is why my body trembles and fearfulness stirs in the pit of my stomach. From my time in the wild I knew Humbaba. From my time in the mountains I learned the dangers of the Cedar Forest. The trees grow for thousands of miles in every direction; to *[194–215]*

ENEMIES BECOME COMRADES

enter the forest is to meet with menace. Enlil appointed Humbaba as guardian of the cedars. Flames shoot from his mouth and his breath is death and his roar is a floodtide. What makes you want to undertake such a foolish challenge?" Gilgamesh said, "My friend, I will scale the slopes of the Cedar Forest. . . ."

Enkidu cleared his throat. "My friend,
can we really go to the Cedar Forest?
To protect the trees through terror and dread
Humbaba was appointed by Enlil's decree,
    that road is not a road to be taken,
    that man is not a man to be looked at!
He defends the forest, a tireless guardian;   220
Humbaba—his voice is a raging torrent,
his mouth is the fire god, his breath is death.
Across hundreds of leagues he hears the cries
of the forest—who would dare disturb its depths?
Second only to Adad, god of the storms,   225
who among the Igigi has courage to oppose him?
To guard the cedars as a fearsome presence
is Humbaba's destiny, by order of Enlil.
Who enters the forest will be seized by madness."
Gilgamesh collected his thoughts to speak: 230
"Enkidu, listen to what I say.
Why do you talk like a coward, my friend?

Your words are weak, you disturb my heart.
The days of humankind are numbered,
all man's achievements are nothing but a wind, 235
his accomplishments will cease to exist.
You were born and you grew up in the wilds of the plains,
lions feared you, you learned nature's laws;
wherever you went men would flee and hide.
Your heart is wise and battle hardened. 240
Come, my friend, let's go to the forge."
The two of them made their way to the smithy,

[243–246]

The blacksmiths were discussing the work at hand.

They forged tremendous axes, each weighing more than [248–259] a hundred pounds. They cast great swords, with each blade weighing more than a hundred pounds, and the hilts weighing thirty pounds, inlaid with a further thirty pounds of gold. Gilgamesh ordered the seven gates of the city be closed and bolted, and summoned his people. Gilgamesh was seated on his throne in the main square while the crowd gathered around him to hear to his words.

"Listen to me, young men of this land; 260
brothers of Uruk, skilled in combat.
I have grown in boldness to travel distant roads

and stride into battle, uncertain of the outcome.
I will head out on a dangerous path;
give me your blessing so I might depart 265
then return home safely to see your faces,
enter the Gate of Uruk with pride.
I will oversee the Festival of New Year—
it will happen twice in the same year!
Start the celebrations, begin the revelries, 270
let the drums rumble before Ninsun 'She-Wild-Cow.'"
Enkidu appealed to the elders of Uruk
and the young fighting men, skilled in battle.
"Tell him not to enter the Cedar Forest.
The road that goes there is not to be walked. 275
The man who lives there is not to be seen.
Humbaba—his voice is a raging torrent,
his mouth is the fire god, his breath is death.
Across hundreds of leagues he hears the whispers
of the forest—what fool would disturb its depths? 280
Second only to Adad, god of the storms,
who among the Igigi has courage to oppose him?
To guard the cedars as a fearsome presence
is Humbaba's destiny, by order of Enlil.
Who enters the forest will be seized by madness." 285
The chief advisor rose to his feet
and gave Gilgamesh the benefit of his wisdom.

"You are young, Gilgamesh, and led by your heart.
You do not know what your words mean.
Humbaba—his voice is a raging torrent,
his mouth is the fire god, his breath is death.
From miles away he listens to the trees—
who enters the forest will be seized by madness.
What fool would venture into its depths,
who among the Igigi could oppose Humbaba,
second only to Adad, god of the storms?
To guard the cedars as a fearsome presence
is Humbaba's destiny, by order of Enlil."
Gilgamesh listened to the chief advisor,
he looked in Enkidu's direction and smiled.

Gilgamesh said, "Do I look frightened? Do I seem afraid? Shall I be called a coward forever? No, my friends. I will follow the path to the Cedar Forest and fall on Humbaba like a lion. I will penetrate deep into the woods, cut timber from the sacred forest, fell mighty trees. Then I will build a raft, and when I have severed Humbaba's head from his shoulders, I will put it on board and sail it downstream."

TABLET III

May the Gods Protect

The elders of Uruk offer advice for success in the mission. Ninsun, the mother of Gilgamesh, makes offerings to the sun god, Shamash, beseeching him to stand by Gilgamesh during the expedition. She adopts Enkidu as her own son and as brother to Gilgamesh. Gilgamesh commands the people of Uruk to uphold the law during his absence, then the two comrades set off for the Cedar Forest.

"Come back to the harbor of Uruk in good health,
don't rely on your strength alone, Gilgamesh,
be watchful, then deliver the telling blow.
'Who leads the way will protect his comrade—
the pathfinder will prove a shield to his friend.'   5
Let Enkidu walk in front of you on your journey,
he knows the way to the Cedar Forest,
he is battle hardened and a warrior to learn from,
may he keep his companion, his 'double,' safe,
bring him home in one piece to the comfort of his wives!   10
We entrust our king's safety to you, Enkidu,
repay our faith by returning him home."
Gilgamesh cleared his throat to speak,

gathered his thoughts, saying to Enkidu:
"Come, my friend, let us go to the palace 15
of great queen Ninsun 'She-Wild-Cow.'
Astute and ingenious, she is all knowing
and will guide our feet in a wise direction."
The two men clasped hands in comradeship.
Then Gilgamesh and Enkidu went to Egalmah 20
to stand in the presence of the great queen Ninsun.
In audience before her, Gilgamesh stood
and addressed the goddess Ninsun, his mother.
"I have grown in boldness, I can make this journey,
tread the road to the home of Humbaba 25
and face an uncertain battle there.
The path I intend to take is unclear.
Allow me to go—I pray for your blessing.
Let me see your face on my safe return
and enter Uruk with bliss in my heart, 30
and twice perform the Festival of New Year.
Yes, twice in one year I will celebrate New Year—
let that custom be established, let revelries take place.
Let the drums rumble like the Storm God himself!"
Her heart became heavy, Ninsun "She-Wild-Cow," 35
at the words and plans of her son, Gilgamesh.
Seven times she bathed in the house of cleansing,
purified herself with tamarisk and soapwort.

She dressed in a garment that graced her body,
and chose a necklace worthy of her breast. 40
With her finery in place and her crown on her head
she passed through the gathering of women in the temple,
ascended the steps that led to the roof
and prepared to burn incense before Shamash the Sun God.
She scattered her offerings. She lifted up her arms. 45
"You have burdened my son with a restless heart.
You have stirred his thoughts, so now he will travel
the distant road to the land of Humbaba
to enter a battle beyond his understanding.
He is steering a course toward the unknown. 50
From the day he departs till the day he returns,
until he arrives at the Cedar Forest,
until he unseats the monstrous Humbaba,
and slays the evil creature you despise,
as you circle each day around the earth's boundary, 55
may your bride, Aya, take courage and remind you:
'Deliver him safely to the guards of the night.'
Entrust him to protectors as the evening watch begins.*

[59–62]

You open the gates and the herd is released;

---

* It can be assumed that in the missing lines that follow, Ninsun's beseeching of the sun god, Shamash, develops into a litany of praise describing the transformative effect of sunlight at dawn.

for the sake of mankind you advance across the land;
mountains shine in the brightening sky;   65
the cattle on the plains glow red in your radiance;*

[67–71]

crowds assemble at the coming of your light;
the holy Anunnaki bask in your rays.
May Aya, your bride, have the courage to remind you:
'Entrust this man to the guards of the night.'   75
Make a road without hazards for his feet to follow.
Ensure that Enkidu walks in front,
he knows the way to the Cedar Forest.
Let him cross the plains and pass through the mountains.
Put a torch in his hand to light up the path.   80
As Gilgamesh journeys to the Cedar Forest
may the days be long, may the nights be short.
Let his belt be fastened and his footwork secure,
let him pitch a camp to sleep in at dusk.
As evening darkens let him lie down and rest.   85
May your bride, Aya, have the courage to remind you:
'When Gilgamesh and Enkidu enter the battle,
unleash the storm winds, let them howl and rage.'
Southerly, Northerly, Easterly, Westerly,
thrashing wind, evil wind, crushing wind, demon wind,   90

---

* The compliments appear to continue in the missing lines.

the icy blast and the frenzied gust,
>   the sand squall, the hurricane, and the furious gale—
let thirteen winds cloud Humbaba's face!
Let Gilgamesh's weapons reach Humbaba's flesh!
At that time of day when you dazzle and flare
lend some of your rays to the man who reveres you.   95
May your mules then carry you swiftly onward;
a seat and a bed will be made ready,
the brother-gods will bring you bread of your pleasing,
Aya will mop your brow with her dress."
Again Ninsun "She-Wild-Cow" beseeched Shamash: 100
"Will Gilgamesh not be a god one day?
Will he not reside in the heavens with you?
Will he not rest a hand on the scepter of the Moon God?
Or philosophize with Ea, god of the Apsu?
Or lead many races of people in this world?   105
Or dwell with Ningishzida in the Land of No Return?
O Shamash, when he enters the Cedar Forest
he must not fail, he must not fall.*

[109–114]

You are leading him into Humbaba's lair."   115
When Ninsun had made her appeal to Shamash—

---

* Fragmented phrases in the partial lines that follow and the incantatory tone that precedes them imply that Ninsun's ongoing supplications are now framed in the negative, warning of the dangers ahead and perhaps imploring Shamash to discourage the undertaking.

clever and knowing, wise in all ways—
the mother of Gilgamesh kissed the ground,
extinguished the incense, and descended from the roof.
Then she summoned Enkidu and declared her intentions. 120
"Enkidu, you were not a child of my womb.
Now my son's followers will be your family:
the priestesses, devotees, the women of the temple."
She hung sacred pendants around his neck.
"The women of the temple will adopt this man; 125
the Divine Daughters will foster and raise him.
I will love him as a mother would love her son.
Let Gilgamesh treat him as a brother would.

[129–130]

When you journey with Gilgamesh to the Cedar Forest
may the days be long, may the nights be short.
Let your belt be secure, your reflexes sharp.
May a safe encampment guard you at nightfall."*

[135–202]

"From the day we leave till the day we return,
while we make our way to the Cedar Forest

---

* The passage that follows is either lost or extremely fragmentary. It can be assumed Ninsun continues to instruct Gilgamesh and Enkidu in preparation for their journey, and that rituals are performed involving juniper and incense in the hope of securing a safe passage and a successful outcome. When the text becomes legible again, Gilgamesh seems to be issuing orders to the citizens of Uruk regarding their conduct in his absence.

and condemn the fearsome Humbaba to his death 205
and destroy all the evil that Shamash abhors,
remember the words of your ruler, Gilgamesh:
be certain to abstain from disloyal ambitions;
no voice should rally young men in the street.
Be merciful to the weak and prosecute offenders, 210
until like children we achieve our desires
and plant our spears in Humbaba's gate!"
The commanders of Uruk applauded their leader.
The youth of the city ran as one behind him
and officers knelt to kiss Gilgamesh's feet. 215
"Come back safely to the harbor of Uruk.
Gilgamesh, don't trust in your strength alone.
Train your eyes on the target, let your blows hit home.
The man in front will shield his companion,
and protect his friend through his knowledge of the path. 220
Let Enkidu lead the way in this mission,
he knows the tracks through the Cedar Forest.
He is battle hardened and a master of combat.
Allow him to guide you through the mountain passes,
let him steer your course and keep you safe 225
and bring you home to your wives in one piece!
Enkidu, we entrust you with the life of our king;
repay our faith and return him to our fold."
Enkidu considered his reply, and then spoke:

"Gilgamesh, your mind is made up and nothing will dissuade you. So be it. Banish all fear from your heart. And follow where I tread, because I know the way to Humbaba's lair, and the paths he travels inside the Cedar Forest." The crowd cheered, their passions were stirred. The young men shouted, "Go, Gilgamesh, and come back triumphant. May your god stand by your side in battle. May Shamash lead you to victory over Humbaba." Then Gilgamesh and Enkidu began their journey.

[230–240]

TABLET IV

A Journey to War

Gilgamesh and Enkidu journey toward the Cedar Forest, covering the vast distance at superhuman speed. Each day is much like the last, reported through a series of repeated lines and verses. On five occasions when they pitch camp, Gilgamesh has a vivid dream. He reports the details of the visions to Enkidu, and each time they are interpreted by Enkidu as good omens for the fight to come. Shamash advises the pair how to defeat Humbaba.

After forty leagues they stopped and broke bread.
After sixty leagues they stopped and pitched camp.
A hundred leagues in a single day!
Mount Lebanon appeared in the distance before them—
    a six-week trek in only three days.
Facing Shamash the Sun God they dug a well   5
and filled their vessels with fresh water.
Gilgamesh climbed to the top of the mountain
and tipped out roasted flour as a sacrifice.
"Mountain, speak sweetly, bring me a dream."
Enkidu built a house for the Dream God to visit,   10
made a cover at its entrance to shut out the storm,

drew a circle on the floor for Gilgamesh to lie in,
then laid down himself, like a net, by the door.
Gilgamesh rested his chin on his knees
and sleep poured over him, falling from above.
In the middle of the night he roused from his slumber,
rose to his feet, and said to his comrade:
"Friend, did you call me? Why am I awake?
If you did not touch me why am I startled?
Did a god pass by? Why is my skin numb?
My friend, in my sleep I experienced a vision;
the dream I had was strange and confusing.
We had made our camp in a valley in the mountains
when above our heads the mountain collapsed.
And like ants through rubble we scurried away."
The wild-born man gave a thoughtful answer,
explaining the meaning of the dream to his partner.
"The dream you had is a happy one, my friend.
The dream is precious, and a good omen.
The mountain you saw, my comrade, is Humbaba.
We shall trap Humbaba, fight him to the death,
and leave him to rot at the scene of the battle.
At dawn, Shamash will signal his pleasure."
After forty leagues they stopped and broke bread.
After sixty leagues they stopped and pitched camp.
A hundred leagues in a single day!

Mount Lebanon appeared in the distance before them—
    a six-week trek in only three days.
Facing Shamash the Sun God they dug a well
and filled their vessels with fresh water.
Gilgamesh climbed to the top of the mountain   40
and tipped out roasted flour as a sacrifice.
"Mountain, speak sweetly, bring me a dream."
Enkidu built a house for the Dream God to visit,
made a cover at its entrance to shut out the storm,
drew a circle on the floor for Gilgamesh to lie in,   45
then laid down himself, like a net, by the door.
Gilgamesh rested his chin on his knees
and sleep poured over him, falling from above.
In the middle of the night he roused from his slumber,
rose to his feet, and said to his comrade: 50
"Friend, did you call me? Why am I awake?
If you did not touch me why am I startled?
Did a god pass by? Why is my skin numb?
My friend, I experienced a second vision;
the dream I had was strange and confusing."   55

"A mountain was above me, its weight on top of me.   *[56–77]*
When it collapsed it gripped my feet and enveloped
my arms so I could not move. Then like a lion a man
appeared, beautiful and luminous. He reached out for

my hand and pulled me free." Enkidu said, "This is a good omen. The mountain that dragged you down was Humbaba, trying to cripple you with fear and throw you to the floor. But the man who rescued you was Shamash the Sun God. He will stand at your side in your hour of need."

"At dawn, Shamash will signal his pleasure."
After forty leagues they stopped and broke bread.
After sixty leagues they stopped and pitched camp. 80
A hundred leagues in a single day!
Mount Lebanon appeared in the distance before them—
    a six-week trek in only three days.
Facing Shamash the Sun God they dug a well
and filled their vessels with fresh water.
Gilgamesh climbed to the top of the mountain 85
and tipped out roasted flour as a sacrifice.
"Mountain, speak sweetly, bring me a dream."
Enkidu built a house for the Dream God to visit,
made a cover at its entrance to shut out the storm,
drew a circle on the floor for Gilgamesh to lie in, 90
then laid down himself, like a net, by the door.
Gilgamesh rested his chin on his knees
and sleep poured over him, falling from above.
In the middle of the night he roused from his slumber,
rose to his feet, and said to his comrade: 95

"Friend, did you call me? Why am I awake?
If you did not touch me why am I startled?
Did a god pass by? Why is my skin numb?
My friend, I experienced a third vision;
the dream I had was strange and confusing.
The heavens cried and the earth thundered.
The day became dark and deathly still.
Lightning flashed, fires broke out.
Flames shot skyward, death rained down.
Then the blazes dimmed and the fire went out,
fading and fading, turning to ash.
As a man of the wild, share your thoughts with me."
So Enkidu reflected on the meaning of the dream.
"My friend, your dream is a promising one."

"The storm you saw was the rage of Humbaba. The fires and the flames were the anger of Humbaba. But he could not defeat you in battle, not for all his burning fury. Your eyes will shine brighter. Shamash the Sun God will blaze for you, turning Humbaba's weapons to cinders and ash. The time of our glory draws nearer and destiny is on our side." *[110–119]*

After forty leagues they stopped and broke bread.
After sixty leagues they stopped and pitched camp.

A hundred leagues in a single day!
Mount Lebanon appeared in the distance before them—
    a six-week trek in only three days.
Facing Shamash the Sun God they dug a well
and filled their vessels with fresh water.   125
Gilgamesh climbed to the top of the mountain
and tipped out roasted flour as a sacrifice.
"Mountain, speak sweetly, bring me a dream."
Enkidu built a house for the Dream God to visit,
made a cover at its entrance to shut out the storm,   130
drew a circle on the floor for Gilgamesh to lie in,
then laid down himself, like a net, by the door.
Gilgamesh rested his chin on his knees
and sleep poured over him, falling from above.
In the middle of the night he roused from his slumber, 135
rose to his feet, and said to his comrade:
"Friend, did you call me? Why am I awake?
If you did not touch me why am I startled?
Did a god pass by? Why is my skin numb?
My friend, I experienced a fourth vision;   140
the dream I had was strange and confusing.

"The most ominous and vivid dream so far. I watched a   *[142–161]*
Thunderbird above me in the sky, soaring over me like a
cloud, then diving toward me. It was horrifying to look

at. Its breath was death and it spoke flames. Then a man was standing at my side. He seized the Thunderbird, bound its wings, and threw it at my feet. Enkidu, who grew up in the wilderness, you know the meaning of dreams, tell me what this means." Enkidu said, "You watched a Thunderbird above you in the sky, soaring over you like a cloud, then diving toward you. It was horrifying to look at. Its breath was death and it spoke flames. It shone with a fearful light. But Shamash bound its wings and threw it at your feet. He will seize the arms of Humbaba so we will overcome him in battle."

After forty leagues they stopped and broke bread.
After sixty leagues they stopped and pitched camp.
A hundred leagues in a single day!
Facing Shamash the Sun God they dug a well 165
and filled their vessels with fresh water.
Gilgamesh climbed to the top of the mountain
and tipped out roasted flour as a sacrifice.
"Mountain, speak sweetly, bring me a dream."
Enkidu built a house for the Dream God to visit, 170
made a cover at its entrance to shut out the storm,
drew a circle on the floor for Gilgamesh to lie in,
then laid down himself, like a net, by the door.
Gilgamesh rested his chin on his knees
and sleep poured over him, falling from above. 175
In the middle of the night he roused from his slumber,

rose to his feet, and said to his comrade:
"Friend, did you call me? Why am I awake?
If you did not touch me why am I startled?
Did a god pass by? Why is my skin numb?
My friend, I experienced a fifth vision;
the dream I had was strange and confusing."

"As I wrestled with a giant wild bull it bellowed and [183–189] kicked. When it stamped its feet great clouds of dust rose up and darkened the skies. I fell in front of its hooves and couldn't move, but a man reached down toward me, raised me up by my arms, touched my cheek, and put water to my lips. Surely the bull is the monster Humbaba, waiting to trample me?" Enkidu said, "The man who pulled you out from under the bull is radiant Shamash. He will offer his support in your hour of need. And the man who put water to your lips is your father, the god Lugalbanda. He will join us in battle; we will fight the monster Humbaba and we will achieve the impossible."

"Stand firm, offspring of the womb of Uruk,
show Humbaba that the warrior before him
is Gilgamesh, born from the belly of Uruk."
Shamash heard the words from Enkidu's mouth,
and his voice called out from heaven at that moment:
"Hurry, be ready to move against Humbaba.

Do not allow him to engage you in the forest.
Seven battle coats protect him in combat;
take him by surprise, while he wears only one."
They heard a sound from far off in the distance,
like the wildest of bulls rearing and bucking. 200
A terrifying yell echoed through the trees—
the roar of Humbaba, guardian of the forest,
his voice rising to a bellowing din.
Humbaba thundered like Adad, god of storms.

[205–209]

Gilgamesh turned to speak to Enkidu: 210
"Comrade, we are neither weaklings or cowards.
All sons were born to fight, that's the truth."
And Enkidu turned to Gilgamesh in reply:
"The enemy we disturb is something very strange.
Humbaba is like nothing else in this world." 215
And Gilgamesh, in turn, said this to Enkidu:
"My friend, let me slaughter the monster Humbaba."

TABLET V

Death and Destruction

Gilgamesh and Enkidu arrive at their destination and follow a path into the trees. The forest is thick with tall cedars and alive with the calls of animals and birds. The two men support and compliment each other, drawing courage from their alliance and comradeship. Sensing danger, Gilgamesh calls out to Shamash for help. Humbaba's roar booms out across the forest. Shamash directs the thirteen winds into Humbaba's face and Gilgamesh attacks him. Severely wounded, Humbaba pleads for mercy, but Enkidu urges Gilgamesh to deliver the fatal blow. Having slain Humbaba and his sons, the two men fell trees in the forest and make a door from a lofty cedar as an offer of appeasement to the god Enlil, Humbaba's patron.

They gazed in wonder at the great forest,
stared awestruck at the lofty cedars.
They noticed a place to enter the trees
and the track where Humbaba came and went,
a well-trodden passage, straight and clear. 5
Their eyes were drawn to the Cedar Mountain—
court of the gods, seat of the goddesses.
Cedars thrived on the sun-kissed slopes

and the shade they cast was richly perfumed.
Like a matted garment, briars and brambles   10
choked the paths through the trees and thickets.
Saplings of cedar grew for miles to every side,
with tracts of cypresses shooting up beyond them.
The canopy was knitted and knotted with creepers;
sap and resin came raining down   15
and flowed away through channels and gorges.
A bird called out, then the forest echoed
with the racket of more birds calling in answer.
A lone cicada sounded its note,
triggering a chorus of piping and hymning.   20
A turtledove answered the cries of a pigeon.
The forest applauded the rickety stork,
rejoiced at the presence of the francolin.
Infant monkeys howled, their mothers chanted;
like singers and drummers their noisy performance 25
rumbled every day in Humbaba's ears.
The lofty cedars threw their shadows
and in their shade a fear fell on Gilgamesh:
his arms were rigid, seized with cramp,
his legs became lifeless, they felt heavy and limp. 30
Enkidu prepared to speak to Gilgamesh:
"Come, let's penetrate the heart of the forest.
Join hands and we'll raise the battle cry."

DEATH AND DESTRUCTION

Gilgamesh replied to Enkidu:
"Why, my friend, do we cower like weaklings, 35
when we already conquered a mountain range?
A worthy adversary stands before us.
By removing this obstacle we shall see the light.
My comrade, skilled in the art of war,
you are battle hardened and do not fear death. 40
When smeared in blood you do not fear death.
Let the prophet in your mind imagine fury,
let your voice thunder like the deepest drum,
let your arms and legs wake up from their weakness.
Hold me, comrade, and we'll fight as one, 45
focus your thoughts on the fight before us;
forget about death, go hunting for life.
Be astute and alert as you walk in front,
protecting yourself and shielding your ally,
writing your name in the books of history." 50
They arrived together in that distant place,
their words at an end, and stood in silence
marveling in awe at the cedar forest.

[54–72]

Enkidu prepared to speak to Gilgamesh:
"My friend, Humbaba looms before us.
He stands alone, though, and we are two. 75
Two lesser men become stronger together.

Slippery slopes are best scaled in pairs.
Twins will outmuscle the single child.
A rope gains strength when twined with another.
Two cubs can bring down the adult lion. 80
Let our joint stance be our firm foundation.
My friend, an arrow needs a bow to fly.
The road you have taken has brought us to here."

[84–86]

"My friend, call down the winds of Shamash;
commander of gales, summoner of storms,
appeal to the hurricane-bringer Shamash."
Weeping, Gilgamesh looked up toward Shamash, 90
his streaming tears gilded by sunlight.
"Remember that day when I trusted in you.
Stand by me again in my hour of need."
From above Gilgamesh, high in the sky,
Shamash heard the words of the warrior's prayer, 95
and his voice thundered from beyond the clouds.
"Stand bravely against him, block his path,
he must not pass through the grove to his lair
to put on his seven robes of radiance;
he has taken six off and wears only one." 100
In the distance they heard a bone-chilling growl,
like a wild aurochs preparing to charge,
a single pitiless terrifying bellow.

DEATH AND DESTRUCTION

The guardian of the forest's voice boomed out,
shaking the trees of the forest to their roots. 105
Humbaba was roaring like Adad, god of storms.

[107–115]

Humbaba prepared his words for Gilgamesh:
"You dare to approach me, advised by this half-wit.
Come, fatherless Enkidu, spawn of a fish,
crossbred freak of a tortoise and a turtle
who never sucked milk from his mother's tit. 120
I watched you as a youth, but chose not to devour you.
Why lead Gilgamesh to my door like a traitor?
Why stand before me like a foreign enemy?
I will slit his throat and slice open his gullet,
feed him to the ravens and eagles and vultures!" 125
Gilgamesh spoke to his comrade Enkidu:
"Humbaba's face has darkened in anger.
Bravely we marched to his land to destroy him
but a trembling heart won't be calmed in an instant."
Enkidu replied to his comrade Gilgamesh: 130
"Why is your voice now quivering with fear?
You grieve my heart with your simpering mouth.
The challenge is standing directly before us:
the molten copper pours into the mold,
stop stoking the fire and fanning the coals— 135
let the torrent flow. Crack the whip,

don't retreat one step, don't turn your back.
Strike like a lion. Land the first blow.

[139–140]

Keep your father, Lugalbanda, in mind,
let your dreams of victory feed your thoughts."
Gilgamesh was roused by the words of his friend.
The mountain shattered as he pounded the bedrock.
Like a savage lion he launched his attack 145
and Enkidu sprang like a wild cat.
At the heart of the forest he grabbed Humbaba,
tore off his cloaks of protection with his hands,
scattered them in pieces between the trees.
In rage and fury Humbaba bellowed: 150
"I will smash them against the roof of the sky,
I will dash them against the floor of the world."
He lifted them up but the sky was too high,
he threw them down but the ground was too low.
The ground split open beneath their heels. 155
The summits of Lebanon shattered as they spun,
clouds that were white in the sky turned black
and a death-like mist descended upon them.
Then Shamash summoned the mighty storm winds:
Southerly, Northerly, Easterly, Westerly, 160
thrashing wind, evil wind, crushing wind, demon wind,

the icy blast and the frenzied gust,
>   the sand squall, the hurricane, and the furious gale.
Thirteen winds lashed Humbaba's face
till he could not gore and he could not buck.
Then Gilgamesh's weapons laid him low. 165
Humbaba pleaded with Gilgamesh for mercy:
"You are young; you are still your mother's child,
the offspring of Ninsun 'She-Wild-Cow,'
by the will of Shamash. Son of the mountains,
flower of Uruk, you are Gilgamesh the King. 170
A corpse never served his master well
but a living slave brings profit to his lord.
Show compassion, Gilgamesh, and save me from death.
Let me go on living to answer your wishes:
all the lumber you ask for I will happily fell; 175
for you I will guard the incense trees.
Your palace will be proud of my gifts of timber."
Enkidu addressed his comrade Gilgamesh:
"My friend, don't be swayed by Humbaba's words,
his supplications will soften your mind. 180
If you free him now our lives will be erased.
He will lash us to a tree in the Cedar Forest,
he will put on his seven cloaks of protection."
Humbaba heard the words of Enkidu.

He lifted his weeping face toward Shamash, 185
his tears flowing in the rays of the sun.*

[187–189]

"You understand the workings of my forest, 190
you have learned the power of words and language.
I should have hung you from a sapling at the border,
fed you to the ravenous vultures and eagles;
my fate now rests entirely in your hands.
Persuade Gilgamesh not to send me to my death." 195
Enkidu turned to his comrade Gilgamesh:
"My friend, kill Humbaba, ruler of the forest;
slay the ferocious guardian of the cedars,
finish him now, bring an end to his power
before Enlil the almighty hears of our deed. 200
Our plan of action will enrage a great god:
Enlil in Nippur, Humbaba's patron.
Be the hero of a story that will echo through time,
how Gilgamesh ended Humbaba's existence."
Humbaba heard what Enkidu had said. 205
He raised his head and prepared to speak:

"When Enkidu roamed the countryside and lived among [207–248]
wild creatures I never harmed him, I never stained the

---

* In the missing lines that follow, Humbaba petitions for his life, addressing Enkidu.

DEATH AND DESTRUCTION

hillsides with his blood. Shamash, stand before me in judgement, be my witness. No woman gave birth to me, no man was my father, I was born to the mountain, raised by the mountain, nurtured by your light. Enkidu, your words in the ear of Gilgamesh can spare my life." Enkidu said to Gilgamesh, "Slay Humbaba, kill the monster who is an enemy of your god, Shamash. Why pity him, why show him mercy?" Gilgamesh said to Enkidu, "Victory is within our grasp, his powers are deserting him, his auras turn to mist, his seven protections flee into the trees."

Then Enkidu spoke, saying to Gilgamesh:
"My friend, catch a bird then hold it tight. 250
Let it go and live in fear of its offspring.
You have Humbaba here in your grip;
let him wriggle free and wherever you go
he will go as well with revenge on his mind."
Humbaba heard the words that Enkidu spoke. 255
He lifted his head and wept before Shamash,
his tears flowing in the rays of the sun.
"Enkidu," he pleaded, "you entered the forest,
with clashing weapons of war, like a prince,
bringing hostilities to the lord of this house. 260
Now Gilgamesh, a shepherd, waits on your word,
like a hireling willing to obey your orders.
My freedom rests entirely on your lips:
instruct Gilgamesh to spare my life."

Enkidu spoke, saying to Gilgamesh: 265
"My friend, kill Humbaba, guardian of the forest.
Slay him, slaughter him, end his reign.
Comrade, bring death to the keeper of the cedars
before Enlil the almighty learns our intentions
and the rage and anger of the gods is raised. 270
Let history be yours, let eternity tell
how Gilgamesh dispatched the fearsome Humbaba."
Again Humbaba heard the words of Enkidu
and lifted his weeping face toward Shamash,
his flowing tears golden in the radiance.* 275

[276–277]

"May they never return to the land of their home,
may neither man live to see old age,
may Enkidu have no gravedigger but his friend Gil-
 gamesh." 280
Enkidu prepared his words for Gilgamesh:
"I speak to you, my friend, but you do not listen.
For as long as he lives he spits out curses;
let him choke swallowing his poisonous words."
Gilgamesh heard the voice of his friend. 285
He drew the dirk from its sheath at his side
and plunged the blade in Humbaba's neck.

---

* In the two missing lines that follow, Humbaba's appeals for leniency appear to have turned into prayers of revenge.

DEATH AND DESTRUCTION

Enkidu cut out his heart and his guts.
Jumping up to Humbaba's head
he hacked off the tusks and took them as trophies. 290
And blood rained down all across the mountains.
And intestines spewed all across the mountains.

[293–299]

Gilgamesh went rampaging through the forest, 300
felling cedars for incense as an offering to Enlil.
Then Enkidu prepared to speak to Gilgamesh:
"My friend, we have flattened tracts of the forest,
how will we answer to Enlil in Nippur?
With the skill of a warrior you slayed its guardian 305
then tore down trees in a fit of rage."
Afterward they butchered Humbaba's seven sons:
the Cricket, the Screecher, the Typhoon, the Shrieker,
    the Wheedler, the Leach, the Storm-Devil—all murdered.
Their axes weighed over ten stones each;
every stroke threw up splinters as tall as a man. 310
Gilgamesh got to work, chopping down a tree;
Enkidu looked for the truest cuts of timber
then prepared to speak, saying to Gilgamesh:
"My friend, we have toppled a towering cedar
whose crown reached into the very heavens. 315
Let us fashion a door six rods in height,
    two rods in width, all carved from one piece.

The Euphrates shall carry it to the House of Enlil;
in the sanctuary of Nippur the people will rejoice."
With boughs of cedar and cypress branches
they constructed a raft tightly bound by creepers   320
and loaded on their kit. Ready to steer,
Enkidu took hold of the rudder at the stern.
Gilgamesh boarded with Humbaba's head.

TABLET VI

A Fatal Rejection

The two men return to Uruk. Impressed with Gilgamesh's heroism and attracted by his beauty, the goddess Ishtar asks for his hand in marriage. Gilgamesh says he would be a fool to accept, listing her acts of cruelty and humiliation against her former lovers and husbands. Grievously insulted, Ishtar demands that her father, Anu, send the Bull of Heaven in revenge. Gilgamesh and Enkidu slay the Bull, and Enkidu threatens Ishtar with a similar fate. Ishtar performs funeral rites for the Bull and determines that Gilgamesh should experience sorrow for his actions. Gilgamesh and Enkidu celebrate their triumph, but in his sleep Enkidu has a troubling dream.

He washed his weapons and his matted hair,
let his locks unfurl across his shoulders,
threw his torn and filthy clothes aside,
and dressed in a robe tied off with a sash.
Then Gilgamesh lifted his crown to his head.   5
Ishtar was watching, gazing at his beauty.
"Gilgamesh, say you will be my bridegroom,
I insist you offer me the gift of your fruits.
You shall be my husband, I shall be your wife.

A gold and lapis lazuli chariot is yours,   10
with gilded wheels and amber horns,
harnessed to storm beasts and giant mules.
Enter the cedar-scented temple;
when you cross the threshold to this sacred house
both doorway and throne shall kiss your feet.   15
Let kings and lords bow low before you
and offer you tributes from the mountains and the fields.
May your she-goats bear triplets and your ewes twins
and your pack mule outpace the wild donkey
and your chariot horses gallop with pride   20
and your yoked oxen be the ploughman's envy."
Gilgamesh opened his mouth to speak,
saying these very words to Ishtar:
"If I were to take your hand in marriage,
who would wash my clothes and cleanse my body,   25
who would satisfy my hunger and quench my thirst?
Would you feed me bread, fit for a god?
Would you pour me beer, fit for a king?
What possible sacrifices should I offer?
What treasure or gifts should I pile high?   30
What splendid cloak should I wrap myself in?
Why would I want to take you as my wife:
you're a frost without the power to freeze,
a door that lets in the wind and the cold,

a palace where warriors are put to the sword, 35
an elephant that buries men in its dung,
a bitumen that blackens those who touch it,
a waterskin that dribbles all over its owner,
a boulder that blunders through stone walls,
a battering ram in the enemy's hands, 40
a shoe that bites the foot that wears it.
Which of your husbands lasted forever?
Which of your warriors made it to heaven?
Allow me to list your former lovers,
like the nameless one whose arm you plucked off, 45
and Dumuzi, your husband in younger days,
condemned to reside with the dead forever.
You loved the crowned and vibrant hoopoe
until you beat him and broke his wing;
now he sits in the woods, crying and flightless. 50
You loved the lion, that epitome of strength,
but hollowed out several pits to impound him.
You loved the stallion, that battle-proud creature,
but controlled him with whips and spurs and spikes
and galloped him hard over seven miles 55
and forced him to drink from muddy water
and sentenced his mother to a lifetime of tears.
You loved the shepherd, the musterer, herdsman,
who devotedly stacked and lit fires for your meals

and slaughtered young goats for you every day 60
till you struck him and turned him into a wolf,
then his own shepherd boys chased him away
and sheepdogs sank their teeth in his thighs.
You loved Ishullanu, your father's gardener,
who loyally gifted you baskets of dates 65
and brought joy to your table every day;
you set him in your sights, went to his door:
'Ishullanu, come, let me taste your strength.
Let your hand tend my forbidden places.'
Ishullanu the gardener answered the goddess: 70
'Why me? Do you really ask this of me?
I have already eaten my mother's bread,
why would I swallow these vulgar taunts?
Me, clothed in rushes against the cold.'
You listened to every word he said 75
then struck him and turned him into a frog
and made him squat in the garden of his making,
a frog that can't jump and can't swim either.
And you would love me as you loved them?"
When Ishtar heard the words of Gilgamesh 80
she flew into a rage and went up to heaven.
In front of Anu, her father, she wept.
Before Antu, her mother, her tears flowed.
"Father, Gilgamesh slanders and defames me.

A FATAL REJECTION

Over and over he abuses and offends me, 85
insulting my name and my reputation."
Anu prepared his thoughts before speaking,
saying these words to Ishtar, his daughter:
"But did you not quarrel with King Gilgamesh?
Did you not tease and provoke him yourself, 90
until he reacted with sneers and jibes?"
Ishtar prepared her thoughts before speaking,
saying these words to Anu, her father:
"Father, give me the Bull of Heaven.
Let me slay Gilgamesh in his own stronghold. 95
If you refuse me the Bull of Heaven
I will smash the walls of the underworld
and open the gates that imprison the dead,
so the dead shall rise up and eat the living,
and the dead shall outnumber and overrun the living." 100
Anu collected his thoughts before replying,
saying these words to Ishtar, his daughter:
"Before I can grant you the Bull of Heaven
the widows of Uruk must gather up hay
for seven years, and the farmers grow grass." 105
Ishtar prepared to speak in reply,
saying these words to Anu, her father:
"What fodder is required I stored already.
What harvests are needed I made happen.

The widows gathered hay for a full seven years 110
and the farmers of Uruk sowed and reaped.
Let vengeance be mine through the rage of the Bull."
Anu listened to the words of his daughter
and placed in her hands the Bull's nose rope.
She came from the skies, leading it onward. 115
When the Bull strutted into the kingdom of Uruk
reed marsh and forest fell into drought
and the river sank seven cubits when it drank.
When the Bull snorted a crater opened up
and a hundred young men toppled into the hole. 120
When it snorted again a new crater appeared
and two hundred young men tumbled into its depths.
When it snorted once more a third crater appeared
and Enkidu fell in, up to his waist.
Leaping out he seized the Bull by its horns 125
but the Bull spat drool and slobber in his face
and hurled its dung with its powerful tail.
Enkidu gathered his words to speak,
saying to his comrade Gilgamesh:
"My friend, we declared ourselves heroes of this city, 130
so how shall we prove ourselves to the crowd?
I have felt the power of the Bull of Heaven,
experienced its strength, sensed its intentions.
I will test its might and muscle again

by approaching the Bull of Heaven from the rear. 135
I will seize the beast by the thick of its tail.
I will hobble its heels by standing on its hooves.
I will hold it steady with my own weight
while you, like a butcher, skilled in the art,
plunge a knife in the kill spot behind its head." 140
Enkidu crept up on the Bull from behind
and seized it by the thickest part of its tail,
then stood on its heels, with his knees in its thighs,
so the Bull was disabled by Enkidu's weight,
and Gilgamesh, like a slaughterman, practiced and
   precise, 145
drove his knife through the spine between horns and neck,
and sent the Bull of Heaven to its death.
They held up its heart and offered it to Shamash.
They bowed their heads respectfully to Shamash
then sat down together, the two comrades. 150
Ishtar went up on the wall of Uruk,
she stamped her feet and wailed in distress.
"Gilgamesh has slain the Bull of Heaven,
the man who mocked me." Enkidu, in response,
threw the Bull of Heaven's intestines at Ishtar. 155
"Be grateful I don't do the same to you.
If I catch you I will drape your shoulders with its guts."
Ishtar summoned her attendants and priestesses;

by the body she performed a funeral rite.
Gilgamesh called for his craftsmen and smiths,   160
who marveled at the size of the creature's horns:
lapis lazuli—thirty pounds in weight
and hard and thick around the rims—
they could each hold hundreds of gallons of oil.
They would serve to anoint his god, Lugalbanda;   165
he would hang them both in the chamber where he slept.
In the River Euphrates they cleansed their hands,
then clasped each other and went on their way.
As they rode through the streets of Uruk-the-Sheepfold
the people assembled to cheer them on their way.   170
Gilgamesh called to the maids in his service:
"Who is Uruk's most handsome hero,
who is Uruk's most magnificent man?"
"Gilgamesh is Uruk's most handsome hero.
Gilgamesh is Uruk's most magnificent man.   175
The Bull of Heaven fell foul of his rage;
no person on the street takes his name in vain,
no citizen of Uruk stands in his way."
In Gilgamesh's palace celebrations took place
until tiredness called every person to their bed.   180
As he slept, a dream entered Enkidu's mind;
when he woke he revealed the details of his vision,
saying to Gilgamesh, "What does this mean?"

TABLET VII

A Death Foretold

Enkidu dreams that the gods have assembled to decide his fate. In a feverish state he addresses the door made from cedar that was offered to Enlil, angry that it failed to ensure his safety. He curses the hunter and Shamhat, who brought about his transformation from wild creature to civilized human, though at the calming and consoling words of Shamash he retracts his condemnation. On his deathbed he experiences another dream, a disturbing vision of the Netherworld that is a portent of his destiny. His sickness worsens, he wishes that he had died a warrior's death in battle, and he passes away.

"Why are the great gods assembled, my friend?"

"In my dream the gods Anu, Enlil, Ea, and Shamash came together in council. Anu spoke to Enlil, saying, 'Gilgamesh and Enkidu have slain Humbaba, guardian of the Cedar Forest, and killed the Bull of Heaven, so one of them must die.' Enlil replied, 'Gilgamesh must not die. Spare him and take Enkidu's life.' Shamash said to Enlil, 'In both matters they acted at my command, when they killed Humbaba and slaughtered the Bull of Heaven. They had my blessing, so why should Enkidu die? Enkidu, who obeyed my orders and is innocent?' At [2–36] which Enlil became angry, saying, 'You marched at their side, you fought with them, you are an accomplice in both killings.'" As Enkidu recalled his dream he became stricken with fear and grief. "O my brother, Gilgamesh. The gods will take me from you, we will never be together again, I will reside forever with the dead. I will cross the threshold into the Netherworld and never see my beloved brother again."

In his mind's eye he saw the great door,
and spoke to the door as if it could hear him.
"Door of the forest, lacking all awareness,
I possess wisdom which you never could. 40
I searched for your timber for forty leagues
till I finally came to the giant cedar,
peerless among the trees of the forest.
Door, you stand six rods in height,
    two rods in width, one cubit deep,
your pole and pivots are all of one piece. 45
I made and lifted you, hung you in Nippur,
and is this the reward for my efforts, Door?
Is this how you show your gratitude, Door?
I should raise an axe and cut you down,
ship you like a raft to the Shining Temple, 50
downstream to the Shining Temple of Shamash,
to stand in the gate of the Shining Temple,

with fearsome Thunderbirds guarding the entrance.
Let the Door hang at the portal of the palace,
let the Door stand firm in Shamash's city, 55
and in Uruk let Shamash's name be sung,
because Shamash listened in my hour of need,
gave me a weapon in the time of battle.
I built you, Door, I lifted you upright,
I can lay you flat and break you into pieces. 60
May a future king hate the sight of you,
or pin you by your hinges in some dark corner,
replace my name with his own and be cursed."
He tore at his clothes, threw his robes to the ground.
And he wept at the sound of his own words. 65
Gilgamesh heard the anguish of his friend
and in no time at all his own tears were flowing.
Gilgamesh spoke, saying to Enkidu:
"My friend, it is clear this dream has disturbed you.
Has your sensible mind become deranged? 70
Why does sacrilege issue from your heart?
The dream was vivid, with many omens,
your sleeping lips were like buzzing flies.
The vision was deep and your terror real,
but the one who lives is the one who wails; 75
the dead bequeath sorrow to those who survive.
Let me offer prayers to the great gods,

let my supplications find your god Shamash.
In your presence I will plead with the father-god, Anu,
and beseech Enlil, the divine advisor.   80
Let Ea look kindly on my appeals.
I will cast a statue of you in gold,
its scale beyond measure, priceless in value.
But friend, no payment of precious metal
can reverse the word of Enlil once spoken.   85
His commandments are law and never erased.
He will not withdraw a single syllable.
My friend, our destinies have been decided;
some lives must end early, as fate decrees."
At the very first rays of morning light   90
sorrowful Enkidu looked up toward Shamash,
his tears shining in the glow of dawn.
"Hear me, Shamash, as my life fades away.
As for that hunter—the trapper who found me—
who led me to live in the shadow of my friend,   95
let him live in the shadow of his own friend!
Let poverty strike him, let his wages dwindle,
let his profits be nothing before your eyes.
May the gods fly out of the window of his house!"
And once he had truly cursed the hunter   100
he turned his anger on Shamhat the courtesan.
"Shamhat, I will prophesize your destiny in life,

a fate to endure till the end of your days.
I will damn you, Shamhat, with a powerful curse,
a hex to take hold this very instant. 105
May you never reside in a sumptuous dwelling;
may you never have the love of your own family;
may you never enjoy the companionship of women;
may your beautiful dresses be fouled by mud;
may the drunkard smear dirt on your festive costume; 110
may a house of beautiful ornaments elude you;
may your lands be puddled into clay by the potter;
may you never possess the table or chairs
to hold a great feast and seat your guests;
may the bed you make love in be nothing but a plank; 115
may you sit at the crossing of dusty highways;
may a ruined wall be your chamber and shelter;
may thorn and bramble pierce your feet;
may the drunk and the sober slap your cheek;
may a lady of standing bring a claim against you; 120
may the builder leave a hole for the rain in your roof;
may an owl roost in the room where you sleep;
may a banquet never be served in your hall;

[124–129]

You took my purity and made me weak; 130
in my wild homeland you drained my strength."
Shamash the Sun God heard his curses

and a voice rang out from heaven at that moment.
"Enkidu, why turn your anger on Shamhat,
who fed you bread, the food of gods, 135
who poured you beer, fit for a king,
who clothed your body in the fine garments
and made you a comrade of mighty Gilgamesh?
Now, Gilgamesh, your friend and brother,
will lay you down on a royal bed. 140
On a bed of great honor he will lay you down.
You will lie in rest on his left-hand side
and the lords of the Netherworld will kiss your feet.
He will make the people of Uruk mourn you,
he will make the wealthy bereft with sorrow. 145
At your death he will wear his hair unwashed
and roam the outlands in a lion's pelt."
On hearing the words of valiant Shamash
Enkidu's raging heart grew calmer;
Enkidu's furious heart grew quiet. 150
"Shamhat, let me wish a new destiny for you;
my mouth cursed you but now let it praise you.
May governors and nobles be smitten with love.
From two leagues away, may men slap their thighs,
and shake out their locks from four leagues away! 155
May soldiers not hesitate to unfasten their belts!

A DEATH FORETOLD

May obsidian, gold, and lapis lazuli
be your gifts, along with countless earrings.
May ingenious Ishtar find you a man
who will open the doors of his treasure house for you   160
and abandon his wife—a mother of seven!"
His mouth rambled, his mind was sick,
he lay on his bed with his thoughts wandering.
From the core of his body he spoke to his friend:
"Gilgamesh, what a dream I had last night.   165
The heavens cried out and the earth answered,
with me in their midst, between sky and land.
I saw a man with a haunting expression,
his face like the face of the Thunderbird,
with the claws of a lion and the talons of an eagle.   170
He overpowered me and grabbed my hair—
reared up like a magic rope when I struck him.
When he struck me back I sank like a reed raft,
then he trampled my body like a wild bull
and I flailed about in his venomous drool.   175
I screamed for help. 'Rescue me, friend.'
But you were afraid and kept your distance.

[178–181]

His next blow transformed me into a dove
and he bound my arms like a trussed bird,

led me to Irkalla's house of darkness,
along the passageways of no return 185
to the place that nobody ever leaves,
a dungeon where prisoners plead for light,
whose meals are dirt and whose bread is clay,
whose clothes are not clothes but the feathers of birds,
who spend their days in total blackness. 190
The lock on the door was clogged with grime;
a silence fell on the House of Dust.
And when I entered the House of Dust
I saw the crowns of monarchs piled high,
and saw the ancient kings of the land 195
who once honored Anu and Enlil with banquets,
offered them bread, poured them cool water.
And seated there in the House of Dust
were the sacred lords and the high priests,
and the holy clerics and ministers, 200
anointers, attendants, adherents, acolytes,
and there sat Etana, and there sat Shakkan,
and Ereshkigal, Queen of the Netherworld,
with her scribe, Belet-seri, squatting at her feet,
holding up a tablet and reading to the sovereign. 205
Seeing me approach, Ereshkigal raised her head:
'Who leads this man to the door of the dead?

A DEATH FORETOLD

Who brings this man into our dominion?"*

[209–250]

"Me, who endured every suffering with you
and marched at your side. Never forget me."
"Yours is a dream that cannot be ignored;
the dream happens and your strength disappears."
Enkidu fell sick for one day, then a second, 255
lying on his bed, too weak to rise.
On the third and fourth day the sickness worsened,
and worsened again from the fifth day to the tenth,
the malady sapping his will and his senses.
On the eleventh day and again on the twelfth 260
he lay on his bed in the grip of the illness,
and called to Gilgamesh with a failing voice:
"My god has turned against me, my friend.
I wish I had died at the heart of a battle.
No matter how much I feared the fight 265
to fall in combat is a glorious end,
but mine is not a warrior's death."

---

* A segment of more than forty missing lines follows; when the text resumes, it seems that Enkidu has finished recalling his dream and is in conversation with Gilgamesh from his deathbed.

TABLET VIII

A Grief Laid Bare

Gilgamesh is distraught with sorrow. He orders that an effigy be created in Enkidu's image, made of costly materials. He performs funeral rites for Enkidu, places treasures with the body, and makes offerings to the gods, beseeching them to take care of his beloved friend in the afterlife. A ceremonial feast is prepared.

In the light of dawn, as morning broke,
Gilgamesh wept for his dead friend.
"Enkidu, a wild gazelle was your mother,
and a wild donkey of the hills your father;
you were reared on the milk of the wandering herds,   5
taught by beasts to seek the best pasture.
Enkidu, may the paths of the Cedar Forest
echo in mourning, night and day.
May the elders of Uruk-the-Sheepfold mourn you.
May the crowds who praised our exploits mourn you.   10
May the highest peaks of the mountains mourn you.
May the streams weep and their tears run pure.
May the meadows mourn you as a mother would,
may the boxwood, cedar, and cypress mourn you

in the woods we stole through with murder in mind. 15
May the bear, hyena, leopard, and lynx,
    the deer, cheetah, tiger, and wolf,
the lion, aurochs, stag, and wild goat
    all mourn your passing with the creatures of the fields.
May the pure waters of the River Ulay,
    whose banks we strutted on, mourn your name.
May the sacred Euphrates flow in lament,
whose water we poured from skins as libation. 20
May the young men of Uruk-the-Sheepfold weep,
who watched us battle the Bull of Heaven.
May the farmer weep in his furrowed field,
who sang your praises as he worked the plough.
May the streets of bustling Uruk mourn you, 25
and the floodplains honor you with their rich silt.
May the shepherd in his sheepfold mourn you,
   who sweetened
beer and butter and milk for your mouth.
May the shepherd boy cry his tears of loss
who smeared your lips with irresistible ghee. 30
May the brewer in the brewery weep for you,
who concocted drafts of ale to your taste.
May the women of the temples weep for you,
who anointed your head with scented oils.
May the groom weep in the wedding chapel 35

like a husband mourning the loss of a wife.
May the carefree young folk of Uruk mourn you;
the boys grieving your death like your brothers,
the girls untying their hair like your sisters.
May mothers and fathers mourn you, Enkidu. 40
And on that day, I will mourn you too.
Hear me, young men, hear my grief.
Hear me, elders of sprawling Uruk.
I will cry in sorrow for Enkidu my friend,
like a funeral woman I will mourn bitterly. 45
Enkidu my axe, my trusty arm,
the sword in my sheath, my protecting shield,
my festival robe, my belt of plenty:
an evil wind has robbed me of you.
My friend, who is now a shooed-away mule, 50
a wandering donkey, a leopard in the wild,
we leaned on each other, scaled the mountains,
we seized and slaughtered the Bull of Heaven,
we felled Humbaba of the Cedar Forest.
What kind of sleep has taken you away? 55
Your mind is elsewhere, you are deaf to my words."
Enkidu did not lift his head.
Gilgamesh touched his lifeless heart
and covered his face like a veiled bride
and circled around him like a soaring eagle. 60

Like a restless lioness whose cubs are stolen
he paced about, turning this way and that.
He tore out hanks of his curly hair,
ripped off his finery and threw it to the floor.
In the light of dawn, as morning broke, 65
Gilgamesh issued an order to his country:
"Stonecutter. Coppersmith. Goldsmith. Jeweler.
Construct a statue in Enkidu's image."
In his mind he visualized the effigy of his soul mate.
"My friend, with your limbs of precious metal, 70
your eyebrows of shining lapis lazuli,
> your limbs and body of gleaming gold,*

[72–83]

I will put you to rest on a great bed,
on a well-prepared bed I will lay you out. 85
You will sit in comfort on my left-hand side,
the lords of the Netherworld will kiss your feet.
I will make the citizens of Uruk weep,
and the wealthy shall feel the emptiness of sadness.
I will wear the matted locks of mourning, 90
I will roam the wilderness in a lion's pelt."

---

* The ten or so partially reconstructed lines that follow describe bouts of self-destructive behavior during fits of grief. Gilgamesh tears out his own hair and rips off his clothes.

A GRIEF LAID BARE

In the light of dawn, as morning broke,
Gilgamesh went to his coffers and strongboxes,
breaking the seals and retrieving his treasure:
obsidian, carnelian, conch, alabaster, 95
exquisite jewelry skillfully worked,
and set them aside as offerings to his friend.*

[98–130]

He slaughtered fattened oxen and fattened sheep,
    and piled them up in honor of his friend.
"These gifts I display, O Shamash, for my friend."
Then meat was offered to the lords of the Netherworld.
He made an offering to the great queen Ishtar,
fashioned from the hardest and most sacred wood— 135
and set down his offering to her before Shamash.
"May the great queen Ishtar receive this gift,
may she welcome my friend and walk by his side."
A costly and beautifully threaded robe
he offered to Aruru, and set it before Shamash. 140
"May the great queen Aruru receive this gift,

---

* The missing thirty-three lines that follow are only partly recovered, a frustration since they clearly describe an inventory of fabulous objects that Gilgamesh is "placing" for his friend. The text includes the impressive size and weight of many items, and the materials they consist of, often gold but also ivory, carnelian, and iron. Some would seem to be articles of jewelry or ceremonial ornaments ("shaped like an aurochs," "a scepter"); others are mighty weapons or pieces of armor, such as a quiver, a mace, and a belt.

may she welcome my friend and walk by his side."
A wonderfully worked lapis lazuli flask

[144]

he offered to Ereshkigal, and set it before Shamash.   145
"A gift for the queen of the crowded Netherworld,
may she welcome my friend and walk by his side."
A flute of exquisitely cut carnelian
he offered to Dumuzi, and set it before Shamash.
"Ishtar's beloved shepherd, receive this,   150
welcome my friend and walk at his side."
A throne of dazzling lapis lazuli
and a stunning lapis lazuli scepter
he offered to Namtar, and set it before Shamash.
"Namtar, Angel of Death, receive this,   155
welcome my friend and walk at his side."

[157–158]

... he offered to Hushbishag, and set it before Shamash.
"Hushbishag, warden of the Netherworld, receive this,   160
welcome my friend and walk at his side."
He commanded the smiths to spare no detail;
bindings of silver and bangles of copper
he offered to Qassa-tabat, and set them before Shamash.
"Qassa-tabat, sweeper of the Netherworld, receive this;   165
be a friendly face as you stroll with my friend,
may his heart be strong and his spirits never fail."

A GRIEF LAID BARE

A quiver for his arrows, carefully crafted,
inlaid with carnelian and lapis lazuli
and arranged in the image of the Cedar Forest   170
he set before Shamash and offered to Ninshuluh-hatumma.
"Housekeeper of the Netherworld, receive this gift,
be a friendly face as you stroll by his side,
may his heart be strong and his spirits never fail."
A double-edged dagger with a hilt of lapis lazuli   175
as blue as the blue of the sacred Euphrates
he offered to Bibbu and set it before Shamash.
"Bibbu, slaughterman of the Netherworld, receive this,
welcome my friend and walk at his side."
A priceless flask of translucent alabaster   180
he set before Shamash and offered to Dumuzi-abzu.
"Scapegoat of the Netherworld, receive this,
welcome my friend and walk at his side."*

[184–210]

When Gilgamesh heard this final pronouncement
he shut down his heart, like the damming of a river.
And then, at the very first light of dawn,

---

* In the two dozen or so missing lines that follow, more lavish offerings are made to various deities to secure Enkidu hospitality and companionship in the afterlife. When the poem resumes, we cannot be certain what Gilgamesh is responding to, though reference is made to "the judge of the Anunnaki," the Anunnaki being the deities of the underworld in this context, perhaps confirming Enkidu's death as irreversible.

he allowed his heart to open its floodgates:
he called for a huge elammaku-wood table; 215
he filled a carnelian bowl with honey,
poured ghee in a lapis lazuli dish.
He displayed the decorated table to Shamash;
he presented his marvelous offerings to the sun.

TABLET IX

The Lost Soul

Gilgamesh roams the wilderness, in mourning for the death of his friend and distressed by the realization of his own mortality. Seeking Uta-napishti, who was granted the gift of eternal life and who lives at the end of the world, he arrives at the two-headed mountain guarded by the Scorpion People. The He-Scorpion points out the road ahead; through the night Gilgamesh must run beneath the mountain in complete darkness in a race against the sun. He emerges on the other side in a spectacular garden where trees and bushes are made of precious stones and their flowers are jewels.

Gilgamesh wept for his friend Enkidu,
crying bitter tears as he roamed the land.
"Must I die too, just as Enkidu died?
Sorrow has pierced me right to the core.
Afraid of death I wandered through the wilderness,   5
seeking Uta-napishti, son of Ubara-tutu.
I found the road and went swiftly along it,
arrived at a pass through the mountains in the night
where lions prowled, filling me with terror.
I lifted up my head and prayed to Sin,   10
appealed to the luminous light of the moon,

saying, Sin, protect me, save me from death."
Then Gilgamesh woke from the depths of a dream
and was glad to be alive in the moon's glow.
He reached for his axe and raised his arm, 15
drew a dagger from his belt and raised his arm
then fell on the prowling lions like an arrow,
striking and killing, scattering the pride.

He wore the pelts of the lions and he ate their flesh. He *[19–36]*
dug wells where the earth was dry and drank from the
water. Like a madman he chased the wind but could not
catch it. Shamash the Sun God was troubled by this pitiful behavior. From above he spoke to Gilgamesh, saying,
"Why do you wander through the wilderness like this.
Everlasting life can never be found, so end your search."
Gilgamesh said to Shamash the Sun God, "I will have all
eternity to rest in the Netherworld once my wanderings
are done, so why stop now? Let me see the brilliance
of your light, because in death darkness is endless. Let
me see the glory of the sun while I can." He traveled on
toward the Mountains of Mashu.

The place was famous for its twin summits,
and he came at last to the two-headed mountain
which guards the sun as it rises each morning,
whose peaks touch the very foundations of heaven, 40
whose footings reach into the Netherworld.

THE LOST SOUL

Scorpion People stood sentry at the gate,
with expressions of dread, with deathly features,
whose aura and presence were pure terror.
From dawn to dusk they defended the sun. 45
Gilgamesh's face grew dark with fear
but he gathered his thoughts and cautiously
   approached them.
The He-Scorpion called to the She-Scorpion:
"Who comes toward us, with the flesh of gods?"
The She-Scorpion answered the He-Scorpion: 50
"He is two-thirds god and one-third human."
The He-Scorpion shouted at Gilgamesh,
aimed words at this king, this flesh of the gods.
"What distant road has brought you here?
Which map have you followed to arrive at this gate? 55
How did you ford the treacherous rivers?
Tell me the name of your own country.
In which direction are you now heading?
Inform me if you have a route or plan."*

[60–74]

"I am seeking my forefather, Uta-napishti, 75
who stood in the great assembly of gods,
who knows the secret of life and death."

---

* In the next fourteen missing lines, their conversation continues with Gilgamesh replying to the He-Scorpion.

The He-Scorpion spoke to Gilgamesh,
warned him of the dangers of the journey ahead.
"To succeed, you must be a man like no other;   80
no person has traveled through the heart of this mountain,
a road as deep as the night is long
where no light pierces the smothering darkness"

[84–124]

"Through sorrow and heartache I have pushed forward,   125
my face ravaged with sunburn and frostbite.
Through exhaustion and hardship I have kept going,
so now you must tell me how to reach my goal."
The He-Scorpion considered his reply
and spoke to King Gilgamesh, this god made flesh: 130
"Go, Gilgamesh, the road stands waiting.
May the Mountains of Mashu allow you safe passage.
May the peaks and summits watch over your journey,
may they harbor and protect you along the way,
may the gate of the mountain open wide before you."   135
Gilgamesh listened to the He-Scorpion
and the words he spoke were joyful to his ears;
he set out on the road of the sun at once.
For the first hour Gilgamesh sprinted ahead,
into heavy darkness, where no light entered,   140
blind to whatever came behind him.
For the second hour Gilgamesh sprinted ahead,

into heavy darkness, where no light entered,
blind to whatever came behind him.
For the third hour Gilgamesh sprinted ahead, 145
into heavy darkness, where no light entered,
blind to whatever came behind him.
For the fourth hour Gilgamesh sprinted ahead,
into heavy darkness, where no light entered,
blind to whatever came behind him. 150
For the fifth hour Gilgamesh sprinted ahead,
into heavy darkness, where no light entered,
blind to whatever came behind him.
For the sixth hour Gilgamesh sprinted ahead,
into heavy darkness, where no light entered, 155
blind to whatever came behind him.
For the seventh hour Gilgamesh sprinted ahead,
into heavy darkness, where no light entered,
blind to whatever came behind him.
For the eighth hour Gilgamesh hurried like a river, 160
into heavy darkness, where no light entered,
blind to whatever came behind him.
In the ninth hour the north wind came to meet him,
brushing his face, and he sprinted ahead
into heavy darkness, where no light entered, 165
blind to whatever came behind him.
In the tenth hour of running at full speed

his senses told him he was very close.
In the eleventh hour there was one hour to go.
By the twelfth hour Gilgamesh had outrun the sun, 170
and surfaced ahead of its dazzling brilliance.
Right then he entered the Garden of the Gods.
A carnelian tree was heavy with fruit,
hung with grapes, gorgeous to gaze at.
A lapis lazuli tree was in leaf, 175
with fruit on its boughs, beautiful to the eye.

[177–183]

A cypress tree sparkled, studded with gems,
and a giant cedar glittered with jewels, 185
and wore bark of pappardilu stone
and sasu stone needles and sea-coral cones,
and instead of brambles and thorns there were crystals.
The carob tree he touched was abashmu stone
with bark of subu stone and hematite. 190
Like the stars in the sky above the plain
the garden sparked with rubies and turquoise,
and petals and blossom shone like seashells.
Having raced through the long dark tunnel of night
Gilgamesh wandered in wonder through the brightness. 195
A woman looked up and noticed the stranger.

TABLET X

To the Edge of the World

From the shore beyond the garden, the goddess Shiduri, an innkeeper and brewer, spots the disheveled Gilgamesh and runs to the roof in fear. Gilgamesh explains his plight and his desire to find Uta-napishti. Eventually she points him in the direction of Ur-shanabi, the boatman of Uta-napishti, and his "crew," the Stone Oarsmen. True to character, Gilgamesh wades into battle, destroying the Stone Oarsmen and thereby inadvertently making his own journey more difficult. Ur-shanabi advises Gilgamesh to make punting poles from felled timber so they can cross the Waters of Death. They set sail. On the far shore Gilgamesh meets Uta-napishti.

Shiduri was an innkeeper on the coast,
she lived in a tavern where the land meets the sea,
owned cauldrons and vessels and golden vats.
Her head was hooded, her face was veiled.
Gilgamesh came wandering out of the distance   5
draped in a pelt, a startling sight.
The blood of the gods flowed through his body
but deep within him there was sorrow in his heart
and he wore the face of a weary traveler.

The innkeeper cautiously watched his approach.
She spoke to herself, choosing her words,
taking advice from the voice inside her.
"No doubt this stranger is a bloodthirsty hunter;
out of nowhere he heads directly for my home."
When she saw him coming she barred the gate
and bolted the door and ran to the roof.
But his hearing was good, he heard the commotion;
he lifted his head and looked toward her,
he sent his words in her direction.
"Lady, why shut me out of your tavern,
blocking my way, retreating to the roof?
I will shatter the lock, break down the door."

[23–24]

Shiduri spoke to Gilgamesh:
"For my own safety I barred the gate.
In fear of my life I fled to the roof.
Stay where you are and tell me your story."
Gilgamesh then replied to Shiduri:
"Enkidu was my friend, my comrade in arms.
Shoulder to shoulder we scaled the peaks,
seized and slaughtered the Bull of Heaven,
destroyed Humbaba of the Cedar Forest
and slayed lions in the mountain passes."
Shiduri replied to Gilgamesh, saying:

"If the two of you caused Humbaba's downfall,
destroyed the guardian in the fortress of his forest
and slayed the Bull that descended from Heaven,
and if you butchered lions in the mountains,
then why is your face so sunken and hollow   40
and your body frail and your spirit broken?
Why does your heart seem shadowed with sorrow,
your expression that of a weary traveler,
your face weathered by sunburn and frostbite?
Why roam the wilds in a lion's pelt?"   45
Gilgamesh spoke to Shiduri the innkeeper:
"Why shouldn't my features be sunken and hollow,
my body frail and my spirit broken?
Why shouldn't my heart be shadowed by sorrow,
my face that of the weary traveler,   50
my face weathered by sunburn and frostbite?
Why shouldn't I roam the wilds like a lion?
I mourn for Enkidu, the galloping mule,
the mountain donkey, the leopard of the plains,
who I loved deeply, my brother in hardship,   55
my constant companion through struggles and sickness,
who met the end that all men must face.
I wept for six days and seven nights,
refused to hand over his body for burial
till a maggot came crawling out of his nose.   60

I was suddenly afraid for my own life.
So I roam the wilderness, terrified of death.
My friend's passing was too heavy to bear
so I wandered the steppe on distant roads.
Enkidu's demise was a weight on my heart 65
so I trailed through the grasslands on lonely paths.
How can I ever be quiet or calm
when the friend I loved has turned to clay?
Enkidu, who I loved, has become clay.
Am I just like him? Will I lie down one day 70
not to rise again for eternity?"
So said Gilgamesh to the innkeeper Shiduri.
"Now show me the road to Uta-napishti.
If the way is secret, reveal it to me now.
Give me the bearings, point out the landmarks, 75
I will cross the ocean if the ocean can be crossed.
If not, I will wander the wilderness forever."
The innkeeper replied to Gilgamesh:
"Gilgamesh, not since the days of old
has anyone journeyed across that sea. 80
The hero Shamash sailed over those waters;
no one but Shamash has managed that voyage.
The passage is narrow, the waves are perilous,
and the Waters of Death lie in between.
Gilgamesh, even if you pilot the ocean 85

how will you navigate the Waters of Death?
But look, Gilgamesh, over there is Ur-shanabi,
    boatman of Uta-napishti the Distant,
cutting cedar in the forest with the Stone Oarsmen.
Approach him and let him see your face;
if the crossing can be made then sail with him,   90
if not, then turn and leave for home."
When Gilgamesh had heard Shiduri's words
he reached for his axe and raised it aloft
and drew the dagger from the sheath on his belt
and crept toward them and stormed into action.   95
Like an arrow in battle he fell among them.
Cries rang out from the heart of the forest.
Ur-shanabi, dressed in the aura of his armor,
lifted his battle-axe and everything trembled.
But Gilgamesh bludgeoned him around the head   100
and pinned his arms across his chest.
The Stone Oarsmen—who did not fear
the Waters of Death—put out in the boat.
But Gilgamesh waded into the waves
and hauled back the boat with the Stone Oarsmen   105
and smashed them and tipped them into the river,
then tied the boat to the bank with a rope
and sat at the side of the water to rest.
Then Gilgamesh spoke to Ur-shanabi:

"You raised your axe and made everything tremble,   110
came at me in combat, but I will not fight you."
Ur-shanabi replied to Gilgamesh:
"Your cheeks are hollow and your face is sunken
and your body frail and your spirit broken.
Why does your heart seem shadowed by sorrow,   115
your expression that of a weary traveler,
your face weathered by sunburn and frostbite?
Why roam the wilds in a lion's pelt?"
And Gilgamesh replied to Ur-shanabi:
"Why shouldn't my features be sunken and hollow,   120
my body frail and my spirit broken?
Why shouldn't my heart be darkened by sorrow,
my face that of a weary traveler,
my face weathered by sunburn and frostbite?
Why shouldn't I roam the wilds like a lion?   125
I mourn for Enkidu, the galloping mule,
the mountain donkey, the leopard of the plains:
shoulder to shoulder we scaled the peaks,
seized and slaughtered the Bull of Heaven,
destroyed Humbaba of the Cedar Forest   130
and slayed lions in the mountain passes.
My friend, who I loved, my brother in hardship,
my constant companion through struggles and sickness,
who met the end that all men must face.

I wept for six days and seven nights, 135
refused to hand over his body for burial
till a maggot came crawling out of his nose.
I was suddenly afraid for my own life.
So I roam the wilderness, terrified of death.
My friend's passing was too heavy to bear 140
so I wandered the steppe on distant roads.
Enkidu's demise was a weight on my heart
so I trailed through the grasslands on lonely paths.
How could I ever be quiet or at peace
when the friend I loved has turned into clay? 145
Enkidu, who I loved, has become clay.
Am I just like him? Will I lie down one day,
not to rise again for eternity?"
Gilgamesh said to Ur-shanabi the boatman:
"Which course shall I steer to Uta-napishti, 150
which bearings shall I take? Tell me the way.
What landmarks exist to navigate by?
I will cross the ocean if the ocean can be crossed.
If not, I will wander the wilderness forever."
Ur-shanabi replied to Gilgamesh: 155
"You have stalled your journey with your own hands.
You have smashed the Stone Oarsmen to smithereens,
tipped them in the river, and the cedar is not cut.
Gilgamesh, lift up the axe by your side,

go to the forest, cut three hundred poles   160
of five rods in length; strip them of bark,
carve handles at one end, then carry them here."
Gilgamesh heard Ur-shanabi's words;
with one hand he raised his axe in the air
and drew the dagger from his belt with the other.   165
In the forest he cut three hundred poles,
stripped them of bark, carved their handles,
and carried them back to the boat as instructed.
Then Gilgamesh and Ur-shanabi went aboard
and set out to sea, no crew but themselves.   170
For a journey that takes a month and a half
they had reached the Waters of Death by day three.
Then Ur-shanabi said to Gilgamesh:
"Now punt with the first pole, but do not touch
the Waters of Death, or your hand will be paralyzed.   175
And now punt with the second and the third and the fourth.
And now punt with the fifth and the sixth and the seventh.
And now punt with the eighth and the ninth and the tenth.
And now punt with the eleventh and twelfth poles,
   Gilgamesh."
And so it continued, until no poles were left.   180
Then Ur-shanabi undid his robe
and Gilgamesh tore off his shirt,
so their arms made masts and their clothes made sails.

On the opposite shore Uta-napishti was watching,
listening to the sound of his inner voice, 185
turning things over in his mind.
"Why are the Stone Oarsmen not aboard?
Who is that figure that is not its captain?
I see Ur-shanabi is in the boat
but the man at his side is no one I know. 190
The longer I look the more I am certain
the figure on board is no ordinary human."*

[193–206]

Gilgamesh spoke to Uta-napishti:
"Long live Uta-napishti, son of Ubara-tutu,
who survived to tell of the Great Flood,
of the rising water which coursed through the land 210
and swept away everything in its path."
Uta-napishti spoke to Gilgamesh:
"Your cheeks are hollow and your face is sunken
and your body frail and your spirit broken.
Why does your heart seem shadowed by sorrow, 215
your expression that of a weary traveler,
your face weathered by sunburn and frostbite?
Why roam the wilds in a lion's pelt?"
And Gilgamesh replied to Uta-napishti:

* In the missing lines that follow, Gilgamesh has landed on the far shore and climbed the bank from the quayside.

"Why shouldn't my features be sunken and hollow, 220
my body frail and my spirit broken?
Why shouldn't my heart be darkened by sorrow,
my face that of a weary traveler,
my face weathered by sunburn and frostbite?
Why shouldn't I roam the wilds like a lion? 225
I mourn for Enkidu, the galloping mule,
the mountain donkey, the leopard of the plains:
shoulder to shoulder we scaled the peaks,
seized and slaughtered the Bull of Heaven,
destroyed Humbaba of the Cedar Forest 230
and slayed lions in the mountain passes.
My friend, who I loved, my brother in hardship,
my constant companion through struggles and sickness,
who met the end that all men must face.
I wept for six days and seven nights, 235
refused to hand over his body for burial
till a maggot came crawling out of his nose.
I was suddenly afraid for my own life.
So I roam the wilderness, terrified of death.
My friend's passing was too heavy to bear 240
so I wandered the steppe on distant roads.
Enkidu's demise was a weight on my heart
so I trailed through the grasslands on lonely paths.
How could I ever be quiet or at peace

when the friend I loved has turned into clay? 245
Enkidu, who I loved, has become clay.
Am I just like him? Will I lie down one day
not to rise again for eternity?"
Gilgamesh continued, "So I told myself
I would find the famous and faraway man, 250
and began my journey through distant lands.
I went back and forth over treacherous mountains,
time and again I crisscrossed the oceans.
My face was a picture of sleeplessness,
my spirit was tortured by bitter tiredness, 255
my muscles ached with the pain of heartbreak,
and what did that anguish ever accomplish?
The innkeeper fled from my tattered clothing,
I killed bears, hyenas, lions, leopards,
tigers, stags, wild goats, many creatures, 260
to eat their flesh and wear their skins.
Now slam the door of sorrow and loss
and seal the entrance with bitumen and pitch.
Never let my grief interrupt the dancing
or my mourning silence the music again." 265
Uta-napishti spoke to Gilgamesh:
"Why are you stricken with lamentation?
You, with the flesh of both gods and humans,
made in the image of your mother and father.

Remember the fable of the fool in the palace: 270
they built him a throne and told him to sit,
but his bowl was filled with dregs, not ghee,
and they fed him with rusk and chaff, not bread,
and instead of fine robes they dressed him in rags,
and instead of a belt he was girdled with rope, 275
all because he had no council to guide him,
no advisers to whisper wisdom in his ears.
Gilgamesh, learn a lesson from that story.

[279–296]

You strove and labored but achieved nothing.
You drove yourself onward but without profit.
You strained every nerve and sinew with effort
yet brought the day of your death even closer. 300
Every family tree can be snapped like a reed:
the handsome boy, the beautiful girl,
how suddenly death can spirit them away.
Death appears from nowhere, acts without warning.
No one has seen the face of death. 305
No one has heard the voice of death,
the silent, invisible, savage assassin.
There comes a time when we build a house;
there comes a time when we fill the nest;
there comes a time of feud between heirs; 310
there comes a time of hatred in the land.

There came a time of high water and flood;
one moment the dragonfly followed the river,
its face lit by the light of the sun,
then suddenly everyone and everything was gone.   315
The missing and the dead—how alike they are.
Neither can draw an image of death.
The dead never say good morning to the living.
At the great assembly of the Anunnaki,
the goddess Aruru decreed man's fate: 320
the gods will give and take away life
and no man will know when death will strike."

TABLET XI

The Hardest Lesson to Learn

Uta-napishti relates the story of the Great Flood and his own immortality. The gods had ordered the deluge as retribution for human wrongdoing. They took a vow of silence but the god Ea secretly advised Uta-napishti to build an ark. Enlil was at first angry that a mortal had survived the destruction, but on taking counsel decreed that Uta-napishti and his wife should live as gods at the edge of the world.

Uta-napishti challenges Gilgamesh to stay awake for a week, a test of his conviction and fortitude, and one that he fails. Before Gilgamesh leaves, Uta-napishti reveals the location of a prickly plant that holds the secret of eternal life. Gilgamesh retrieves the plant from the bottom of the Apsu, but later in his journey a snake steals it from him while he is bathing. With Ur-shanabi he arrives back in Uruk, and repeats the words from the beginning of the poem describing the proportions and formation of his kingdom.

Gilgamesh spoke to Uta-napishti:
"I look at you, Uta-napishti the Distant,
and your bodily form is the same as mine;
you are no different—we are very alike.
I promised myself I would meet you in combat,   5
but in your presence my arm does not move.

How did you meet with the gods of life?"
Uta-napishti replied to Gilgamesh:
"I will share a secret, reveal a truth,
explain the mystery of the gods to you.
Shuruppak is a place you know yourself,
a city that sits on the banks of the Euphrates.
The gods were seated within its walls
when the order was given to unleash the Great Flood.
Their father, Anu, pledged his silence,
as did their counsellor, the hero Enlil,
as did youthful Ninurta, his son,
as did Ennugi, their inspector of waterways.
The god Ea was also sworn to silence
but he whispered their words to a fence and a wall.
"Listen, reed fence, take note, stone wall,
Uta-Napishti, put your ear to the hole.
Citizen of Shuruppak, Ubara-tutu's son,
demolish your house and build an ark!
Forsake all riches, seek survival,
abandon your possessions, be a saver of lives,
store the seed of all living creatures on board.
The dimensions of the vessel you must now build
shall be the same to every side,
with her length and breadth of equal size,
and give her a roof overhead like the Apsu."

THE HARDEST LESSON TO LEARN

I understood, and replied to Ea:
"I agree to follow your advice, my master,
I have listened carefully, I will carry out your word.
But what will I say to the city and its elders?"   35
Ea opened his mouth to speak,
replying with these words to me, his servant.
"When they question you, you must say the following.
'So it seems certain that Enlil hates me.
I must banish myself from the walls of your city,   40
my feet must not tread on Enlil's ground.
I must go and never return from the Apsu
    to dwell with Ea, my master, in his realm.
He will lavish you all with rain from the heavens—
a cloudburst of birds, a downpour of fish—
and at harvest time you will reap your rewards.   45
A hail of bread cakes will fall at dawn!
Showers of wheat he will send in the night!'
As the light of morning began to break
the people began to gather at my gate.
The carpenter was there, carrying his axe,   50
and the reed worker too, carrying his stone,
and the boat builder too, carrying his saw.
Young men came too, to lend their strength,
and the old men as well, with braided ropes.
The rich man had brought a barrel of pitch,   55

the pauper had brought bits and pieces of tackle.
By the fifth day her hull was fully constructed,
an acre in area, ten rods high,
every side of her roof ten rods in size.
I designed her shape, drew her form; 60
from bottom to top I gave her six decks,
and assembled her body from seven sections,
and built nine cabins on each of the decks.
I sank bilge bungs and plugs between her ribs,
found a punting pole and mounted the rowlocks. 65
Three thousand gallons of dry bitumen
    for waterproofing were tipped in the cauldron,
then three thousand gallons of crude tar.
Three thousand gallons of oil went aboard
in addition to the oil that was offered in sacrifice
and two vats of oil that the shipwright stowed. 70
For the laborers I kept on slaughtering oxen
and butchered sheep every single day.
Many types of beer and oil and wine
I poured like a river down the throats of my workers
and they drank like men at the feast of New Year. 75
By sunrise I had finished the caulking and greasing,
and before sunset the ark was finished.
Preparing to sail was an arduous task:
slipway poles were laid under the hull

till two-thirds of the boat was in the water. 80
Everything I possessed I carried aboard:
whatever silver I owned I loaded;
whatever gold I owned I loaded;
I loaded the seed of all living things.
My kith and kin I sent up the gangway, 85
every wild creature, every skilled craftsman.
Shamash had stated the hour of departure:
'When cakes fall out of the morning sky
    and wheat pours out of the sky at night
go aboard the boat and batten the hatch.'
The hour of departure had duly arrived. 90
'In the morning cakes will fall from the sky
and wheat will pour from the sky at night.'
I looked to the heavens, watching the weather,
and the oncoming storm was a terrifying sight.
I went aboard and battened the hatch. 95
To the shipwright Puzur-Enlil, who sealed the door,
I bequeathed my estate and worldly goods.
As the light of morning broke in the east
a black cloud rose above the horizon
with Adad, god of storms, booming inside it. 100
Thunder and lightning marched ahead,
bearing Adad's throne across mountains and plains.
The war god, Errakal, ripped out the moorings;

at Ninurta's footfall the weirs overflowed;
the Anunnaki, in a torchlight procession, 105
spilt flames as they came, setting fire to the land.
The eye of the storm passed over the sky,
and all that was bright became lost in darkness.
Rampaging oxen! The shattering of vases!
A hurricane pounded the country all day. 110
The winds raged and the floodgates opened;
the deluge swept through the people like a battle;
brother was unrecognizable to brother;
in the carnage not one person knew another.
Even the gods themselves feared the flood; 115
they withdrew to the upper heaven of Anu,
curled up together like dogs in the open.
Sweet-voiced Aruru, the Mother Goddess,
wailed and screamed like a woman in childbirth.
'The world is ruined, it has turned to clay; 120
in the council of the gods I made the wrong choice,
spoke unwisely in siding with evil,
agreed to a deluge that destroyed my people.
These were my children, they came from my womb,
and now they roll in the waves like minnows.' 125
The gods of the Anunnaki wept with her,
wailing softly, in tears like her,
their mouths fixed with anguished expressions.

THE HARDEST LESSON TO LEARN

For six more days and seven more nights
the storm howled, flattening the land.
When the seventh day had finally arrived
the storm relented; the deluge had ended.
The swollen ocean that had writhed and thrashed
like a woman in labor grew calm and quiet.
I looked at the clouds—the day was placid
but the people of the world were returned to clay.
The flooded plain was as level as a roof.
Sunlight fell on my face through a vent;
I sank to my knees and began to weep,
tears streaming, flowing down my cheeks.
I scanned the horizon in every direction,
fourteen lands were visible to the eye.
The ark ran aground on Mount Nimush
and the mountain held it tight in its grip;
on day one and two it held the ark fast;
on day three and four it held the ark fast;
on day five and six it held the ark fast.
When morning broke on the seventh day
I released a dove, let it fly free,
and the dove went winging across the water.
But with nowhere to perch it returned to my hand.
I released a swallow, let it fly free,
and the swallow went swooping across the water.

But with nowhere to perch it returned to my hand.
I released a raven, let it fly free, 155
and the raven discovered the waters receding,
found food to peck at and did not come back.
I poured out libations to the four winds,
I offered incense at the peak of the mountain,
set seven and seven flasks in place 160
and piled up cedar and myrtle around them.
Till at last the gods smelt the pungent scent.
Till at last the gods smelt the spicy aroma
and gathered like flies where I made my offering.
Aruru held aloft the fly-shaped jewels 165
that Anu once made her to melt her heart.
'I will wear these gems like a string of beads
around my neck, so as never to forget.
Let the gods congregate around the incense,
but exclude Enlil from receiving this offering; 170
without our consent he caused the Great Flood
and condemned my countless people to disaster.'
Just at that moment Enlil arrived;
he saw the ark and flew into a rage,
furious with the other gods at the gathering. 175
'How has this human escaped with his life?
No man should outlive the Great Flood's destruction.'
Ninurta prepared to speak in reply,

saying these words to the warrior Enlil:
'No one but Ea could have brought this about,   180
he alone knows how everything works.'
Ea opened his mouth to reply
and spoke these words to the great god Enlil.
'Enlil, warrior, wise man of the gods,
you recklessly ordered the waters to rise.   185
Mankind had sinned and had to be punished,
the wrongdoers had to pay for their crimes,
but be neither too soft nor too harsh in judgement.
Instead of inflicting a devastating flood
a lion could have purged the people of this land.   190
Instead of inflicting a devastating flood
a wolf could have terrorized the people of this land.
Instead of inflicting a devastating flood
a famine could have ravaged the people of this land.
Instead of inflicting a devastating flood   195
a war could have plunged the people into turmoil.
I did not disclose the secrets of the gods,
just let Uta-napishti witness a dream,
so judge him now and decide his fate.'
Then Enlil himself came aboard the ark,   200
took hold of my hand and led me ashore
and made my wife kneel down by my side,
stood between us, touched our foreheads to bless us.

'Uta-napishti and his wife were humans till today,
but from now they shall be as we are—gods. 205
They will live far away, where rivers meet the sea.'
And they took us to live where the rivers meet the sea.
But who will convene the gods for you, Gilgamesh?
First, prove your desire for eternal life:
stay awake for six days and seven nights." 210
But as soon as Gilgamesh rested his limbs
sleep breathed over him like a mist.
Uta-napishti the Distant spoke to his wife:
"Look, a young man, whose desire is life,
but who falls asleep in the blink of an eye." 215
The wife of Uta-napishti replied:
"Touch him and bring him out of his slumber.
Let him travel home safely on the road he came by.
Let him pass through the gate to his own lands."
Uta-napishti the Distant spoke to his wife: 220
"Mankind is devious, always looking to deceive.
Bake his daily bread, leave the rations at his pillow,
then mark on the walls the days that he slept."
She baked the loaves, lined them up by his head,
then marked the days of his sleep on the wall. 225
A week went by and the first batch was shriveled,
the second batch leathery, the third batch limp,
and the fourth batch of loaves was stale and white,

and the fifth batch of loaves was stained with mold,
and the sixth still fresh, and the seventh still baking   230
when Uta-napishti shook Gilgamesh awake.
Gilgamesh spoke to Uta-napishti the Distant:
"As soon as sleep had poured across me
you shook me and woke me from my sleep."
Uta-napishti the Distant spoke to Gilgamesh: 235
"Come, count your meals of uneaten bread.
Then you'll know how many days you slept.
The first batch of loaves is dry and shriveled,
the second batch leathery, the third batch limp,
and the fourth batch of loaves is stale and white,   240
the fifth batch moldy, the sixth still fresh,
and the seventh still baking as you woke up."
Gilgamesh spoke to Uta-napishti the Distant:
"How can I continue? Where can I go?
Life's thief has taken hold of my flesh.   245
Death haunts my bed, stalks my chamber.
Death stares me in the face wherever I look."
Uta-napishti spoke to Ur-shanabi the boatman.
"May wharf and wherry scorn your name,
may you pine for the shoreline where you worked and
   walked.   250
But for now, look after the man you brought here,
whose body is tangled in matted hair,

whose flesh is defiled by filthy pelts;
take him to the washhouse and fill the tub,
scrub out the dirt from his skin and scalp,   255
ditch those hides in the currents of the sea,
soak him till his body recovers its sweetness,
tie his hair with a resplendent headband,
dress him in the royal robes he deserves.
Until he returns to his native city,   260
until he reaches the end of his road,
may his clothes be unstained, may they look like new."
Ur-shanabi led Gilgamesh down to the washhouse.
He scrubbed the dirt from his skin and scalp.
He ditched his hides in the currents of the sea.   265
He soaked him till his body recovered its sweetness.
He tied his hair with a resplendent headband,
he dressed him in the royal robes he deserved.
"Until he returns to his native city,
until he reaches the end of his road,   270
may his clothes be unstained, may they look like new!"
Gilgamesh and Ur-shanabi went down to the water,
they launched the boat, a two-man crew.
Uta-napishti's wife spoke to her husband:
"Gilgamesh landed here, broken with exhaustion,   275
what parting gift have you offered to him?"
Gilgamesh raised the punting pole

and steered the boat toward the bank
as Uta-napishti called out his name:
"Gilgamesh, you landed here, broken with exhaustion, 280
it is right that I offer a parting gift.
I will share a hidden understanding with you,
reveal a mystery known only to the gods.
There is a plant, a prickly shrub;
its spiny thorns will spike your skin. 285
If you pluck that prickly plant with your hands
the secret of youth will be yours forever."
As soon as Gilgamesh heard those words
he dug a shaft through the earth's crust
then tied heavy stones around his feet 290
that dragged him to the very bottom of the Apsu.
From the depths he plucked the plant with his hands
then cut himself loose from the heavy stones;
he rose through the water and was thrown ashore.
Gilgamesh spoke to Ur-shanabi the boatman: 295
"This plant I have plucked is the flower of life
by which a man can recapture his youth.
Let me take it home to Uruk-the-Sheepfold
and feed it—as a test—to an old man;
if that old man goes backward in age 300
I will eat it myself and be young again!"
After twenty leagues they broke bread,

after thirty leagues they pitched camp.
Finding a pond that was fresh and clear
Gilgamesh bathed in the cool water.   305
But a snake smelt the perfume of the plant he had plucked;
unseen and in silence it slithered up and stole it,
shedding its skin as it slipped away.
Gilgamesh sat and wept that day,
tears streaming, flowing down his cheeks.   310
He turned to speak to Ur-shanabi the boatman:
"I have labored so hard my arms have no strength
and the blood in my heart has almost run dry;
instead of winning this reward for myself
I have helped the most hated creature on the earth.   315
The shaft I dug will have flooded by now,
the tools I used will be washed away
and all landmarks erased. My cause is lost;
I should never have sailed to that distant coast."
At forty leagues they broke bread,   320
at sixty leagues they pitched camp.
When they reached the heart of Uruk-the-Sheepfold
Gilgamesh spoke to Ur-shanabi the boatman:
"Walk around on the upper walls of Uruk,
inspect the stronghold's solid structure.   325
Aren't its courses composed of kiln-baked bricks?
Were its footings not laid by the Seven Sages?

THE HARDEST LESSON TO LEARN

A thousand acres of dwellings and buildings,
    a thousand acres of gardens and groves,
    a thousand acres of quarries and clay-pits,
    and the Temple of Heaven—five hundred acres.
Behold the extent of Uruk-the-Sheepfold!"

GLOSSARY

Characters in Mesopotamian mythology have changing roles across different regions and time periods. As far as possible they are described here in the context of the poem. Each entry is followed by a notation indicating the tablet number and line number of the place or character's first appearance in the poem.

ADAD   The Storm God. II.225
ANTU   The wife of Anu, mother of Ishtar. VI.83
ANU   The father of the gods, the god of the sky. I.80
ANUNNAKI   Those gods associated with the Netherworld. III.73
APSU   A primordial body of fresh water below the surface of the earth, from where all life-giving springs were thought to arise. III.104
ARURU   The Mother Goddess who created humankind, also referred to as Belet-ili. I.49
AYA   A goddess, the wife of Shamash. III.56
BELET-SERI   The auditor or scribe of the Netherworld,

GLOSSARY

who keeps a record of the number and the names of the dead. VII.204

BIBBU   Butcher and slaughterman to the gods. VIII.178

BULL OF HEAVEN   A giant and destructive mythical animal associated with the constellation of Taurus. VI.94

DUMUZI   A former lover or husband of Ishtar. VI.46

DUMUZI-ABZU   A tutelary goddess worshipped in the state of Lagash. VIII.181

EA   A wise and clever deity, the god of the Apsu. I.50

ENKIDU   A wild creature of the hills and grasslands fashioned from a piece of clay to stand up to the tyranny of Gilgamesh. Following his civilizing by Shamhat he becomes Gilgamesh's beloved friend and comrade. I.103

ENLIL   The god of the earth and humankind, and a ruler of the universe with Ana, Ea, and Aruru. I.242

ENNUGI   A god of irrigation, a member of Enlil's court. XI.18

ERESHKIGAL   The queen of the Netherworld. VII.203

ERRAKAL   A god of destruction and violence. XI.103

ETANA   A former Sumerian king of Kish who became a lord of the Netherworld after his death. VII.202

GILGAMESH   Very possibly a historical ruler of Uruk around 2750 BCE, whose name passed into legend. The eponymous protagonist of the poem, two-thirds

GLOSSARY

god and one-third mortal, the son of the goddess Ninsun and King Lugalbanda. I.3

GREAT FLOOD   A fatal deluge sent by the gods to punish mankind's offensive behavior, of which Uta-napishti was the sole survivor. I.8

HOUSE OF DUST   A dwelling place for the dead. VII.192

HUMBABA   A fearsome creature appointed by Enlil as protector of the Cedar Forest. II.[194–215]

HUSHBISHAG   A member of Ereshkigal's retinue in the Netherworld. VIII.159

IGIGI   Those gods who live in heaven above the clouds. II.226

IRKALLA   The lowest and darkest part of the Netherworld, sometimes depicted as an underground cave. VII.184

ISHTAR   Principal deity of Uruk, daughter of Anu and Antu, the goddess of love, desire, and war. Her rejection by Gilgamesh leads indirectly to the death of Enkidu. I.16

ISHULLANU   One of Ishtar's former lovers, a gardener or planter. VI.64

LUGALBANDA   The father of Gilgamesh, a former king of Uruk. I.35

NAMTAR   An attendant of Ereshkigal and gatekeeper of the Netherworld. VIII.154

NINGISHZIDA   An officer of the Netherworld. III.106

GLOSSARY

NINSHULUH-HATUMMA   Housekeeper or cleaner of the Netherworld. VIII.171

NINSUN   "SHE-WILD-COW"   A goddess, the mother of Gilgamesh. I.36

NINURTA   The god of agriculture, the athletic and youthful son of Enlil. I.104

NIPPUR   An ancient Sumerian city, seat of worship of the god Enlil. V.202

NISSABA   The goddess of grain. I.107

PUZUR-ENLIL   Uta-napishti's boat-builder. XI.96

QASSA-TABAT   A divine servant in the Netherworld. VIII.164

SCORPION PEOPLE   The guards of the tunnel beneath the mountain through which the sun must pass each night. IX.42

SEVEN SAGES   The "Apkallu," a group of demigods responsible for the taming and teaching of humankind before the Great Flood. I.21

SHAKKAN   The god of wild and domesticated animals. I.109

SHAMASH   The Sun God, god of justice, the protector of travelers, Gilgamesh's guardian during his adventures. I.241

SHAMHAT   A priestess in Uruk, often defined as a "temple prostitute," who is sent to civilize Enkidu through sexual seduction. I.140

GLOSSARY

SHIDURI   A goddess of brewing and wisdom who keeps an inn at the end of the world. X.1

SIN   The Moon God. IX.10

STONE OARSMEN   Ur-shanabi's crew, who are unaffected by the Waters of Death. X.88

TEMPLE OF HEAVEN   Also the Temple of Eanna, in Uruk, dedicated to the worship of Ishtar and Anu, who are also considered residents of the sanctuary. I.12

THUNDERBIRD   Also known as Anzu, a giant fire-breathing zoomorphic creature, sometimes depicted with the body of an eagle and the head of a lion. VII.53

UBARA-TUTU   A king of Shuruppak before the Great Flood, the father of Uta-napishti. IX.6

UR-SHANABI   Uta-napishti's boatman or ferryman. X.87

URUK (URUK-THE-SHEEPFOLD)   Gilgamesh's kingdom, an ancient Mesopotamian city, modern-day Warka. I.11

UTA-NAPISHTI (THE DISTANT)   A "Noah" character who survived the Great Flood. The former king of Shurrupak, he was awarded immortality by the gods and lives at the end of the world. Also referred to as Atra-Hasis I.42

WATERS OF DEATH   A fatal stretch of ocean between shores at the end of the world. X.84

NOTES

TABLET I: Gilgamesh the King, Enkidu the Man

I.13, *ramparts as straight as woolen thread*: There is no consensus regarding the meaning of this line, or whether it has been correctly transcribed—to some it reads as "like the shining of copper." Perhaps the walls are as straight as a woolen plumb bob, a length of horizontal wool used to ensure a level course of bricks during construction.

I.21, *Were its footings not laid by the Seven Sages?*: Seven is the poem's magic number, and a significant number in cuneiform text. Very early mathematical exercises deal with the problem of calculating with seven in a sixty-based system. Uruk's foundations were laid by the Seven Sages; Enkidu and Shamhat make love for seven nights, and then for a further seven; Enkidu drinks seven flagons of beer; Uruk has seven gates; Ninsun cleanses herself seven times before praying to Shamash; Humbaba has seven protective auras and seven sons, etc., etc.

I.22, *the Temple of Heaven—five hundred acres*: In the original poem, each of Uruk's three districts—buildings, orchards (or date groves), and clay pits—is said to be one šār in area, and the temple of Ishtar half a šār. "Three šār and a half is the size of Uruk." In this context one šār is possibly an area of about four hundred hectares, for which there is no direct or modern equivalent dimension. More generally šār can also mean totality or a very large number. The area enclosed within the walls of the historic settlement of Uruk (modern day Warka), now a UNESCO World Heritage Site, is given as 2.09 square miles, or 541 hectares.

I.52, *in height he measured eleven cubits*: One cubit was usually thought of as the length of the human forearm, perhaps twenty inches or so in this context, or about half a meter.

I.56, *the length of his leg was half a rod*: A Mesopotamian rod, or nindan, was about six meters.

NOTES

I.60, ***His hair grew in sheaves, like the Goddess of Grain***: Another version of the story includes a line here about his teeth glowing like the dawn.

I.140, **"*Shamhat the courtesan*"**: Shamhat's actual title in Uruk society is a vexed issue in readings of *Gilgamesh*. In the original poem she is a *harimtu*, a word often translated as "harlot," and is identified by some as a prostitute working in the temple. Others have disputed the historical accuracy of such an idea and accorded her the status of priestess, or have allocated her an honored position in an attempt to lend her dignity and agency in the eyes of the contemporary reader. Given what she is required to do in the lines that follow, it seems justified in this context to assume that her role, at least in part, was of a sexual nature.

I.271, **"*you will hold him like a wife*"**: The possibility that Gilgamesh's relationship with Enkidu is a romantic or sexual one is discussed on page xxix of the Introduction.

TABLET II: Enemies Become Comrades

II.63, ***a young passerby, invited to a wedding***: The hasty and convenient appearance of this minor character feels awkward to the contemporary reader. His sudden arrival and his crude role in steering the narrative may have been achieved by smoother and subtler means in the original poem.

II.[116–161], ***until their strength and anger were spent***: Given what we know of Gilgamesh's virility and lust, and given the means by which Enkidu has been civilized, the psychosexual implications of a confrontation between the two men are very dramatic. Hormones and adrenaline appear to be fueling them as much as machismo as they begin to wrestle and fight. The whole encounter reads as a substitute for sexual conquest, out of which Gilgamesh finds a permanent partner, comrade, and soulmate.

II.167, **"*Ninsun 'She-Wild-Cow' spoke to her son*"**: Only occasional snippets have been recovered from the next ten lines, including "bitterly" and "in his gate." Other words and phrases suggest that Ninsun describes Enkidu as a person with "unkempt hair," "born in the wilderness" "without anyone" to call family.

II.191, **"*fearfulness stirs in the pit of my stomach*"**: Of the two, Enkidu demonstrates the greater emotional self-awareness, something of a paradox considering he was recently forged from a lump of clay. At this moment he is overcome by a sense of loneliness, and later he is traumatized by thoughts of his impending death. In contrast, Gilgamesh's kneejerk response to his new friend's isolation is to sug-

NOTES

gest a bloodthirsty adventure. It is not until Enkidu's passing that Gilgamesh registers a sense of sorrow and loss, and even then this is quickly transformed into anxieties about his own mortality. An alternative, more generous interpretation could be that Gilgamesh is offering a means by which the despondent Enkidu might find belonging and glory.

II.[194–215], *"let's travel to the Cedar Forest"*: The Anamus Mountains, now known as the Nur Mountains in southern Turkey, and the extension of their fertile slopes into the ranges of northern Lebanon. In other words, a mappable journey to the west, even if the expedition is presented as fantastical in the poem.

II.[194–215], *"I will scale the slopes of the Cedar Forest . . ."*: The final lines in this passage are unrecovered.

II.223, *"Across hundreds of leagues he hears the cries"*: The poem specifies sixty *beru* (in Akkadian) or sixty *danna* (in Sumerian). This is complicated, because the *danna* is both a measure of time and one of distance, or in some ways a combination of both. It could be described as the distance a person could run in a "double-hour" while maintaining the same speed across the entire day, or perhaps more simply as about 6.5 miles. There is no contemporary equivalent, but once rounded up to an equivalent number, the league (3.45 miles) is a useful stand-in, and being relatively obsolete in relation to the measurement of distance on land it brings with it a sense of the old world.

II.268, *"Festival of New Year"*: This appears to be historically accurate for the period. There were two such festivals, in spring and in autumn, around the time of the equinoxes.

TABLET III: May the Gods Protect

III.1, *"Come back to the harbor of Uruk in good health"*: The elders of Uruk continue speaking to Gilgamesh prior to his departure for the Cedar Forest with Enkidu.

III.92, *"let thirteen winds cloud Humbaba's face"*: The conscription of winds as allies in battle was a common device in poems of the era.

TABLET IV: A Journey to War

IV.1, *After forty leagues they stopped and broke bread*: As with the outlining of Gilgamesh's size, strength, and achievements, the absolute numbers are less important than the idea that something superhu-

NOTES

man is being described, beyond the dimensions and capabilities of regular mortals.

IV.4, *a six-week trek in only three days*: The actual distance between Uruk and a view of the fertile and forested Mount Lebanon range is measurable—in the region of five hundred miles—which provides a literal sense of the scale of the undertaking. And given that no form of transportation is mentioned, it is, presumably, a journey accomplished on foot.

IV.197, *"Seven battle coats protect him in combat"*: Often described as "auras," the seven layers of protection manifested as a form of light or radiance. They are also synonymous with Humbaba's seven sons, later slain by Gilgamesh and Enkidu.

IV.217, *"let me slaughter the monster Humbaba"*: The remainder of Tablet IV, of unknown length, is missing.

TABLET V: Death and Destruction

V.6, the Cedar Mountain: Presumably Mount Anamus in the modern-day Hatay region of southern Turkey. As in a number of world myths, the suggestion is that the pantheon of the gods resides at the summit.

V.53, *marveling in awe at the cedar forest*: The missing lines that follow are too fragmentary to allow for plausible reconstruction, though occasional words and phrases suggest that the two would-be assailants are preparing to fight. Weaponry in the form of swords, axes, and hatchets are referred to. One or two lines seem to imply that Humbaba is not only angered by their presence but offended, perhaps seeing Enkidu's challenge as some kind of betrayal.

V.289, *Jumping up to Humbaba's head*: The first few words of line 289 are missing, so it isn't clear if the actions that follow are performed by Enkidu or Gilgamesh.

TABLET VI: A Fatal Rejection

VI.48, *"the crowned and vibrant hoopoe"*: Transcribed as "allala" or "allallu," a type of bird, in the original text. The ornithologist in me could not resist an intervention at this point; the Eurasian hoopoe may not be the correct species, but its attributes and native territory fit the role nicely.

VI.105, *"the farmers grow grass"*: It isn't clear if the hay and the grass are to fuel the Bull of Heaven in advance of its rampage or, more likely, to sustain the people of Uruk in the aftermath of its devastation.

NOTES

VI.164, *they could each hold hundreds of gallons of oil*: In the poem the weight of the horns is given as thirty *minas* each, one *mina* corresponding to about five hundred grams, so roughly two and a half stone or fifteen kilograms per horn. Their capacity is said to be six *kor* each, the equivalent of 1,080 cubic liters, around 238 imperial gallons.

TABLET VII: A Death Foretold

VII.123, *"may a banquet never be served in your hall"*: In the missing lines that follow, further curses follow, the nature of which can be partly surmised based on an assortment of words recovered from lines 127 to 129, including *purple clothing* and *defiled lap*.

VII.177, *"you were afraid and kept your distance"*: In the missing lines below, the struggle continues.

VII.267, *"mine is not a warrior's death"*: Perhaps as many as thirty lines at the end of this section are missing. For as long as they remain undiscovered we are denied the particular details of Enkidu's passing.

TABLET VIII: A Grief Laid Bare

VIII.18, *"the pure waters of the River Ulay"*: The Ulai River, near the ancient city of Susa, close to the modern-day Iranian border.

VIII.68, *"a statue in Enkidu's image"*: Following Enkidu's death Gilgamesh commissions an effigy in his likeness. Subconsciously it is as though the all-powerful king believes he can remake his dead friend and bring him back to life. The scene also recalls the fact that Enkidu was made from clay. The gods had the gift of bringing Enkidu to life from an inert lump of earth, but for all his riches and strength Gilgamesh has no such power.

VIII.156, *"walk at his side"*: In the missing two lines that follow, another offering is presented.

VIII.215, *a huge elammaku-wood table*: Valuable or rare wood of an unspecified origin.

VIII.219, *marvelous offerings to the sun*: The remainder of Tablet VIII, another twenty or thirty lines perhaps, is lost.

TABLET IX: The Lost Soul

IX.[19–36], *the Mountains of Mashu*: An imaginary mountain range to the west.

NOTES

IX.83, *"where no light pierces the smothering darkness"*: The path Gilgamesh must follow involves a race with the sun as it makes its nighttime journey from dusk to dawn through the interior of the mountain. The text resumes with Gilgamesh speaking.

IX.173, *carnelian*: A semiprecious brownish-red stone.

IX.186, *pappardilu stone*: A black stone with white stripes, probably a band agate. The name means something like "singular shiny one." Together with lapis, carnelian, and other stones it is frequently used in rituals against misfortune.

IX.187, *sasu stone*: A tightly banded black-and-white stone with shades of red, yellow, and green, believed to ensure good relationships between gods and humans.

IX.189, *abashmu stone*: A greenish stone often used in amulets. Known as the "stone of sex-appeal," it protects against the "lurker" demon.

IX.190, *subu stone*: Used as jewelry for goddesses and for seals and amulets. It has been identified as "vitriol," "rock crystal," or "agate" but may also have been made of shell.

TABLET X: To the Edge of the World

X.60, *"a maggot came crawling out of his nose"*: One of the most visceral and vivid descriptions in the whole poem, the maggot crawling out of Enkidu's nostril is a telling symbol of human mortality. It has been made clear a number of times that Gilgamesh is two-thirds god; it dawns on him now that, via the corporeal element of his being, he might be subject to the natural processes that have brought about such revolting decay in the body of his friend. Initially the image suggests a high level of decomposition, encouraging the notion that Gilgamesh has not been able to part with the body of his dead friend, like Achilles with the body of Patroclus, though maggots can develop on a corpse within twenty-four hours, especially in warmer climates. It is also interesting that Gilgamesh chooses to disclose this information to Shiduri, and later in the same tablet to Ur-shanabi and Uta-napishti, when no mention of it was made earlier during the long narration of his grief and mourning (and assuming there was no reference to it in any of the missing lines). Perhaps by holding it back the poem implies Gilgamesh has been tortured by memories of this incident throughout his wanderings, a kind of traumatic flashback he can no longer bear to internalize. His unburdening, then, at this delayed stage, feels like an indication of how broken he is, and how close to defeat.

NOTES

X.278, "*learn a lesson from that story*": In the missing lines that follow, Uta-napishti probably goes on to explain the significance of his parable before turning to the inevitability and mystery of human mortality.

TABLET XI: The Hardest Lesson to Learn

XI.4, "*we are very alike*": Gilgamesh is expressing surprise that a man who has achieved life everlasting and has been elevated to the status of a god, or at least allowed to live as one, should be so human in appearance. Perhaps his observation is ironic, since Gilgamesh is two-thirds god himself. Nevertheless, it must be the case that Gilgamesh is referring to Uta-napishti's general form and shape rather than his size, given the extraordinary dimensions of his own body, as recorded earlier in the poem.

XI.11, "*Shuruppak*": Tell Fara in modern-day Iraq. The ancient city was about twenty miles north of Uruk on the banks of the Euphrates. Its significance here is in relation to Uta-napishti, who was the King of Shuruppak before being warned by Ea to build an ark and leave. The fact that the gods had gathered there testifies to its importance as a sacred site. There is some scientific evidence to suggest that the historical location was subject to extensive flooding.

XI.101, "*Thunder and lightning marched ahead*": Sullat and Hanis in the original, gods of destructive weather, often twinned and usually accompanying Adad.

XI.118, "*Aruru, the Mother Goddess*": As Aruru brought humankind into being, the metaphor is not deployed casually.

XI.143, "*The ark ran aground on Mount Nimush*": Probably the mountain known today as Pir Omar Gudrun in Iraq.

XI.164, "*gathered like flies*": It may seem insulting to describe the gods as flies, or as dogs as they were earlier in the tablet. But the metaphor sheds light on the symbiotic relationship between mortals and deities in the Mesopotamian world. Gods could bestow favor and fortune, but were reliant on human offerings for their sustenance. Deprived of nourishment because of the devastating effects of the Great Flood, they are drawn at once to the aroma of the sacrifice.

XI. 197, "'*I did not disclose the secrets of the gods*'": Ea defends his disloyalty to the gods by claiming that in only whispering to a reed fence and a stone wall he kept his promise of silence, i.e. he did not speak to anyone. It feels like a weak case. However, he goes on to blame Enlil for acting unilaterally and disproportionately in sending the Great Flood, a deluge that very nearly wiped out the whole human race, not just those sinners who had offended the gods with their (unspecified) crimes. Enlil appears partly persuaded by the logic of the argument; he raises the status of Uta-napishti and his wife to that of gods, but also instructs them to live at the far side of the world, beyond the reach of other mortals; deification and banishment in the same pronouncement.

XI.210, *"stay awake for six days and seven nights"*: Even though it feels abruptly introduced in the text, this test of Gilgamesh's suitability for his quest is particularly poetic. Earthly tiredness would seem to question his capacity and candidacy for eternal life. The challenge might also be offered in reference to Uta-napishti's own experience of the Great Flood, which raged for seven nights, perhaps requiring him to remain awake and vigilant.

XI.291, *the very bottom of the Apsu*: The poem does not make clear how Gilgamesh knows the location of this plant or how to retrieve it.

BIBLIOGRAPHY

This is less of a reading list and more a description of the books that have formed an untidy parapet around the edge of my desk for several years now, not as well constructed as the ramparts of Uruk but formidable and occasionally insurmountable in many ways. Chief among these is A. R. George's monumental two-volume, thousand-plus-page *The Babylonian Gilgamesh Epic: Introduction, Critical Edition and Cuneiform Texts* (Oxford University Press, 2003). The publication is a masterwork, overwhelming in its scholarship, its breadth of knowledge, and attention to detail. Anyone working on the poem should be grateful for its existence, and lost without it. Thank you to Professor Stephen Harrison at Corpus Christi College, Oxford, for his help in procuring this very heavy and rightly expensive book. Andrew George's 1999 translation, *The Epic of Gilgamesh* (Penguin Classics), and the 2020 second edition have also been essential guides and helpmates in coming to terms with the original poem, as has Benjamin R. Foster's *The Epic of Gilgamesh: A New Translation, Analogues, Criticism, and Response* (W. W. Norton, 2019). Other bricks in the wall include *Gilgamesh: A New Translation of the Ancient Epic*, translated by Sophus Helle (Yale University Press, 2021); *Myths from Mesopotamia: Creation, The Flood, Gilgamesh, and Others* by Stephanie Dalley (Oxford University Press, 1989); *Gilgamesh: A New English Version*, translated by Stephen Mitchell (Profile Books, 2004); *Gilgamesh: The New Translation*, translated by Gerald J. Davis (Insignia Publishing, 2014); *The Epic of Gilgamesh*, translated by N. K. Sandars (Penguin Books, 1960); *The Epic of Gilgamesh*, translated by Kent H. Dixon, illustrated by Kevin H. Dixon (Seven Stories Press, 2018); *Das Gilgamesch-Epos*, translated by Stefan M. Maul (C. H. Beck, 2005); *Gilgamesh: Translated from the Sîn-Leqi-Unninnī Version*, translated by John Gardner and John Maier (Alfred A. Knopf, 1984); *Gilgamesh Retold*, translated by Jenny Lewis (Carcanet, 2018); *Gilgamesh: The Life of a Poem* by Michael Schmidt (Princeton University Press, 2019); and Jeremy Black and Anthony Green's *Gods, Demons and Symbols of Ancient Mesopotamia: An Illustrated Dictionary* (British Museum Press, 1992). There are now many dozens of incredibly insightful and fascinating websites on all aspects of Assyriology, including Gilgamesh, but the most significant and useful is that of the electronic Babylonian Library, which hosts A. R. George's *Poem of Gilgameš* (2022), with contributions by E. Jiménez and G. Rozzi and translated by Anmar A. Fadhil, Andrew

BIBLIOGRAPHY

R. George, and Wasim Khatabe. This is a regularly updated resource and an indispensable reference work when used in conjunction with other translations.

And thank you again to Jacob Dahl, for the ladders to climb and the view on the other side.

ABOUT THE TRANSLATOR

Simon Armitage is professor of poetry at the University of Leeds and a former poet laureate of the United Kingdom (2019–2029). Previously, he taught poetry at the University of Oxford, the University of Iowa's Writer's Workshop, and Princeton University, among others. He has published over a dozen collections of poetry, beginning with *Zoom!* in 1989. Ten years later in 1999, Armitage was named the United Kingdom's Millennium Poet. In 2004 he was elected a Fellow of the Royal Society of Literature, and in 2010 Armitage was awarded the CBE for his services to poetry.

He is also the author of four stage plays, several poetic television films, libretti, and three best-selling memoirs, as well as the translator of the anonymous Middle English poems *Sir Gawain and the Green Knight* and *Pearl*. The latter won the 2017 PEN America Award for Poetry in Translation. Among the numerous other awards he has won for his poetry are a Forward Prize, an Eric Gregory Award, and the Queen's Gold Medal for Poetry. Born in 1963 in the village of Marsden, he now lives in West Yorkshire in the UK.